THE TRANSFIGURATION

His Church, His Glory, His Image

Otis J. Bush

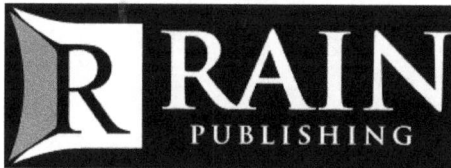

Raleigh, NC

Rain Publishing, LLC
www.rainpublishing.com

Edited by: Sheila Hightower

The Transfiguration
/ Otis J. Bush -- 1st Ed.

ISBN: 978-1-7346106-2-8

Library of Congress Control Number: 2021917986

Dedication

This Book is dedicated to the many wonderful men and women God has raised up in the last four centuries, who He has used to challenge the Church, to rise to new creation realities that Christ paid for in His death, burial, and resurrection.

I acknowledge and appreciate the passion shown by men like Kenneth E. Hagin Sr, Smith Wigglesworth, John G. Lake, George Mueller, Hudson Taylor, and my beloved overseer Bishop James Hash Sr. There is, in every generation, a remnant raised up by our Lord to steer the Church in the direction of the original commission.

Through the many challenges that are hurled at the Church, our Heavenly Father continues to grace her to rise above all and fight the good fight of faith, laying hold of the eternal unseen realm.

This Book, I believe, was inspired to help awaken the reader to a deeper, richer walk with the Creator of the heavens and the earth. It is written to challenge the reader to walk in the deeper realms of the Kingdom so that God can fulfill His purpose in the life of His children as they journey through and on this earth. As the Church nears the end of the age, we see that God's plan is to mature the body of Christ so that we are prepared as laborers of the great in-time harvest. We are also being prepared for the catching away of the Church, so the transformation and the transfiguration process is accelerating because of the quick work God will do in this hour.

We dedicate this work to Him who is working in us all, both to will and to do of His good pleasure.

Hosanna to our King!

Acknowledgements

To our Savior Jesus, who paid the awful ultimate sacrifice for our redemption, we fully acknowledge His Lordship and our salvation. There is nothing that exist without Him. All thrones, dominions, principalities, and power were set forth by Him. We acknowledge the eternal greatness of the fullness of the God head.

I certainly thank God for my loving and devoted wife, Toni Bush, who has been super supportive as I continue to walk towards the calling of God. She has not wavered in her own dedication to the call and words cannot express the treasure God has given me in this wonderful woman of God. I also acknowledge Bishop Hash and Lady Joy, who are true examples of the faith, who have labored in the grace to ensure so many of us were not without the true spiritual supervision ordained by God, that is so needed in this hour. We celebrate and acknowledge so many dear spiritual siblings in Christ who have encouraged, prayed, and supported us in this endeavor of life.

Forward

For several years, I have personally known Pastor Otis Bush—a great man of God with true humility before the mighty King. We have seen people fulfill their destiny through this fresh and pertinent message found in "THE TRANSFIGURATION". This book is a must read book for anyone desiring to grow in Christ and seeking the face of God.

Dr. James C. Hash Sr.
Sr. Pastor/CEO
St Peter's Church & World Outreach Center
Winston Salem, NC 27107

Introduction

Our Father, the Creator of the heavens and the earth, from the very beginning, declared "Let us make man in our image, after our likeness:.." This is a great mystery, and I am now more convinced by the Scriptures than ever, that this man who God had in His heart to create was to eventually be fully complete in Christ Jesus, the Word, that was made flesh. It started in the garden when He made Adam a living soul. This process of the full stature and maturation of redeemed humanity continued after the fall of Adam in the garden. The Scripture declares that Christ was slain from the foundation of the world. This implies to the enlightened that God had a final divine ingredient to place in humanity which included deity. God, through His grace, has given birth to a New Creation with new species born of the incorruptible seed of the Word. We are God's offspring, destined to be like Christ; not only in Spirit as we are now, but we are to receive a spiritual body that is made of the same substance Jesus received during the awesome resurrection power displayed when He was resurrected from both spiritual and physical death. Jesus is the first born of many children. Our Father wants us to grow in the living reality of this Sonship.

Our Father is the Husbandman, and He is building a Kingdom in the earth that is exploding into the fullness of His brightness. The earth shall be filled with the knowledge and the glory of the Lord. There is nothing the enemy of darkness can do to stop the kingdom of light. This is an awakening generation that will, by the grace of God, throw away the knowledge and the ways of the world, counting it all dung for the excellence of the knowledge of Christ. We are not satisfied with the formality and ritualism that has reduced many believers to spiritual blindness by giving them a false identity, luring them into the deception that has plagued humanity since the fall of Adam. We are awakening to the light of the Word that declares Jesus has made us kings and priests unto God.

Prepare to meet your Heavenly Father God on the level of the righteousness of Christ Jesus. Get ready to rejoice evermore in the Good News of the Gospel and the glad tidings of peace! You are the redeemed of the Lord!

Table of Contents

Chapter 1

The Transfiguration of Christ and His Church

God's revealed plan for His Church in these last days is unfolding before us in the progressive revelation of the Scriptures and is being revealed in the events unfolding on the earth. The Father's plan is to mature the Church and transfigure the Church to get it ready for the catching away into the city He has prepared for His children. Jesus said I go away to prepare a place for you that where I am there you may be also. He spoke of returning for His people. "If I go away and prepare a place for you, I will come again and take you to myself, so that where I am you may be also." John 14:3, *Holman Christian Standard Bible*

When Christ ascended to His seated position at the right hand of the Father, He gave gifts unto men. These gifts as noted in the following Scriptures are being used by the Lord God to bring the Church, which is His body, into full maturity.

"Wherefore he saith, When he ascended up on high, he led captivity captive, and gave gifts unto men. (Now that he ascended, what is it but that he also descended first into the lower parts of the earth? He that descended is the same also that ascended up far above all heavens, that he might fill all things.) And he gave some, apostles; and some, prophets; and some, evangelists; and some, pastors and teachers; For the perfecting of the saints, for the work of the ministry, for the edifying of the body of Christ: Till we all come in the unity of the faith, and of the knowledge of the Son of God, unto a perfect man, unto the measure of the stature of the fulness of Christ:" Ephesians 4:8-13

So, the Church is being progressively transformed and transfigured into the fullness of the measure of the stature of Christ as it receives the mature ministry gifts in the body of Christ that will bring forth truth and light supplied by the Spirit of grace (Holy Spirit).

The apostle, prophet, evangelist, pastor, and teacher are the ministry gifts ordained of God for the perfecting of the Church, for the work of the ministry and for the edifying of the Church.

In recent centuries God has raised up men like Count Zinzendorf with the Moravians in Herrnhut, Germany; John Wesley in the Methodist movement; William Seymour in the Pentecostal movement; and with the outpouring of the Holy Spirit that spawned the so-called Spirit-filled churches in the 20th Century throughout the entire world.

Note, that these ministry gifts are ordained by God and not men, nor the religious institutions of men. God Himself, in every generation, has and will continue to raise up ministry gifts that will take the Church to new levels of grace and glory to reach the maturity set for the generation at hand, until the Church reaches rapture-ready perfection. The readiness is based on the finished work of Christ and His being the head over all things to the Church. Ephesians 1:22.

We will elaborate in detail on these gifts in a later chapter.

Right in the midst of this fallen creation, God is transforming the Church and working all things together for our good, that is the good of the Church, His children. In the beginning God created the heavens and the earth. The scripture declares He created the worlds with His words by speaking them into existence. Hebrews 11:3. He calls those things that are not as though they were. He is a speaking Spirit, and we are created in His image, having the same spirit of faith calling those things that are not as though they were. "We having the same spirit of faith, according as it is written, I believed, and therefore have I spoken; we also believe, and therefore speak;" 2 Corinthians 4:13

So, Adam, the first man, was made in His image. He was placed in God's Garden, Eden, and given supreme authority over the works of God's hand in the earth.

God gave Adam a help meet in the garden by taking Eve from His side. They were to rule together over God's creation. See Genesis 2:22. However, through the deception of Satan who borrowed the serpent's body in the garden, Eve was deceived, and Adam disobeyed God by eating the forbidden fruit. "And when the woman saw that the tree was good for food, and that it was pleasant to the eyes, and a tree to be desired to make one wise, she took of the fruit thereof, and did eat, and gave also unto her husband with her; and he did eat." Genesis 3:6

It was through this one act of yielding to the lie of Satan that creation fell. Satan became the God of this world. Adam and Eve died spiritually, and eventually, physically. "And the Lord God commanded the man, saying, Of every tree of the garden thou mayest freely eat:" Genesis 2:16

Man became the servant of both Satan and sin on that unfortunate day; as the scripture says, unto whom you yield your members bodily you become a servant. "Know ye not, that to whom ye yield yourselves servants to obey, his servants ye are to whom ye obey; whether of sin unto death, or of obedience unto righteousness?" Romans 6:16

We are seeing the beginning of the end of all things pertaining to this fallen creation. The original lease given to Adam on the earth is about to expire. The Creator of the heavens and the earth is coming to claim the precious fruit of the earth of whom He has so patiently waited. "Be patient therefore, brethren, unto the coming of the LORD. Behold, the husbandman waiteth for the precious fruit of the earth, and hath long patience for it, until he receive the early and latter rain." James 5:7

So, there will be a massive revival or in gathering of new creatures, men, women, boys, and girls being born again because of the great outpouring of the latter/former rain by the Spirit of God. "Be glad then, ye children of Zion, and rejoice in the Lord your God: for he hath given you the former rain moderately, and he will cause to come down for you the rain, the former rain, and the latter rain in the first month." Joel 2:23 "Then shall we know, if we follow on to know the Lord: his going forth is prepared as the morning; and he shall come unto us as the rain, as the latter and former rain unto the earth." Hosea 6:3. This great harvest of souls is a part of the great transfiguration and maturing of the Church. It is the mature Church that will be used to harvest this massive precious fruit of the earth in this final hour.

The Lord God Jehovah is going to fully restore all of creation. This will include the entire universe. The following Scripture points out the destruction of this fallen creation.

"The Lord is not slack concerning his promise, as some men count slackness; but is longsuffering to us-ward, not willing that any should perish, but that all should come to repentance. But the day of the Lord will come as a thief in the night; in the which the heavens shall pass away with a great noise, and the elements shall melt with fervent heat, the earth also and the works that are therein shall be burned up. Seeing then that all these things shall be dissolved, what manner of persons ought ye to be in all holy conversation and godliness, Looking for and hasting unto the coming of the day of God, wherein the heavens being on fire shall be dissolved, and the elements shall melt with fervent heat?" 2 Peter 3:9-12

So, the Word declares that He will destroy by fire and melt with fervent heat. He also will restore beyond what was in the beginning. The restoration of all things concerning creation is at hand as noted below.

"And he that sat upon the throne said, Behold, I make all things new. And he said unto me, Write: for these words are true and faithful." Revelation 21:5

The Father will bring forth the new heavens and new earth. This will be a completely new creation and completely new creatures (Children of God) who will be like God because even our mortal bodies will be changed in a moment, in the twinkling of an eye! We will pull off mortality and put on immortality, as stated below.

"For this corruptible must put on incorruption, and this mortal must put on immortality. So when this corruptible shall have put on incorruption, and this mortal shall have put on immortality, then shall be brought to pass the saying that is written, Death is swallowed up in victory. O death, where is thy sting? O grave, where is thy victory?" 1 Corinthians 15:53-55

These scriptures are the truths which thrust the Church into the revelation knowledge causing the transfiguration that is needed in these final hours before the catching away of the Church.

The fullness of His salvation will manifest in and upon the Church to empower it to reach the full measure of the stature of Christ. Meaning that the Church in the Book of Acts was in its infancy state. Initially, the early converts didn't understand that the Gentiles were included in God's plan for salvation. An angel appeared to Cornelius, a Gentile, who was a supporter and one who contributed greatly to the cause of Judaism. He told Cornelius to send for Peter who would tell him words by which he and his household would be saved. "There was a certain man in Caesarea called Cornelius, a centurion of the band called the Italian band, A devout man, and one that feared God with all his house, which gave much alms to the people, and prayed to God alway. He saw in a vision evidently about the ninth hour of the day an angel of God coming in to him, and saying unto him, Cornelius. And when he looked on him, he was afraid, and said, What is it, Lord? And he said unto him, Thy prayers and thine alms are come up for a memorial before God. And now send men to Joppa, and call for one Simon, whose surname is Peter:" Acts 10:1-5

The Lord gave Peter a vision on the housetop the day Cornelius's servants arrived to give him a revelation concerning this inclusiveness of the Gentiles, as noted in the following verses:

"On the morrow, as they went on their journey, and drew nigh unto the city, Peter went up upon the housetop to pray about the sixth hour: And he became very hungry, and would have eaten: but while they made ready, he fell into a trance, And saw heaven opened, and a certain vessel descending upon him, as it had been a great sheet knit at the four corners, and let down to the earth: Wherein were all manner of fourfooted beasts of the earth, and wild beasts, and creeping things, and fowls of the air. And there came a voice to him, Rise, Peter; kill, and eat. But Peter said, Not so, Lord; for I have never eaten any thing that is common or unclean. And the voice spake unto him again the second time, What God hath cleansed, that call not thou common. This was done thrice: and the vessel was received up again into Heaven. Now while Peter doubted in himself what this vision which he had seen should mean, behold, the men which were sent from Cornelius had made enquiry for Simon's house, and stood before the gate, And called, and asked whether Simon, which was surnamed Peter, were lodged there. While Peter thought on the vision, the Spirit said unto him, Behold, three men seek thee. Arise therefore, and get thee down, and go with them, doubting nothing: for I have sent them." So, Peter went into Cornelius's house and saw the fulfillment of prophecy concerning the Gentiles receiving Christ as Savior. See Acts 10:24-34.

But as previously stated, this was a newborn church; God and the Holy Spirit came to lead and guide us into all Truth. The continual revelations from these Truths are to guide the Church, until the full transformation and transfiguration into Father God's image which is from glory to glory, is complete; see the noted Scripture below.

"But we all, with open face beholding as in a glass the glory of the Lord, are changed into the same image from glory to glory, even as by the Spirit of the Lord." 2 Corinthians 3:18

Jesus' transfiguration, which took place on the mount as witnessed by the disciples Peter, James, and John, was a shadow and type of how the Church, which is Christ's body, would transform right in the midst of this world's stage – taking on the very image of God in these last days with increased intensity and going from one phase of glory to another.

Let's look briefly at the account in Matthew 17:1-8:

"And after six days Jesus taketh Peter, James, and John his brother, and bringeth them up into an high mountain apart, And was transfigured before them: and his face did shine as the sun, and his raiment was white as the light. And, behold, there appeared unto them Moses and Elias talking with him. Then answered Peter, and said unto Jesus, Lord, it is good for us to be here: if thou wilt, let us make here three tabernacles; one for thee, and one for Moses, and one for Elias. While he yet spake, behold, a bright cloud overshadowed them: and behold a voice out of the cloud, which said, This is my beloved Son, in whom I am well pleased; hear ye him. And when the disciples heard it, they fell on their face, and were sore afraid. And Jesus came and touched them, and said, Arise, and be not afraid. And when they had lifted up their eyes, they saw no man, save Jesus only."

Moses and Elijah appeared on the mountain to witness the Holy declaration of God concerning Christ. The Creator of the heavens descended in a cloud of glory to declare that Jesus, His beloved son, was to be heard above the law and the prophets. Moses represented the law and Elijah represented the prophets. While Jesus communed with Moses and Elijah, Peter spoke of building three tabernacles to represent Moses, Elijah, and Jesus. God spoke volumes when He declared on the Holy mountain, "While he yet spake, behold, a bright cloud overshadowed them: and behold a voice out of the cloud, which said, This is my beloved Son, in whom I am well pleased; hear ye him." Matthew 17:5-6

The Father of our Lord and King declared the dawning of a new age of grace, power, and glory. It was the Kingdom of God coming forth in great power in the manifested Word, made flesh.

The transfiguration of Jesus on that mountain was a prelude to what was to happen to His body which is the Church in these last days. The Church will reach full stature and maturity before the catching away of God's children. "Then we which are alive and remain shall be caught up together

16

with them in the clouds, to meet the Lord in the air: and so shall we ever be with the Lord." 1 Thessalonians 4:17

Darkness will surely increase in the earth, but the light will be greater and greater because of the glorious continual transfiguration of the Church. This light will be demonstrated in the level of truth the Church will walk in, and in the level of God's power that will be seen upon them. We see Daniel prophetically speaking of the end time Church.

"But thou, O Daniel, shut up the words, and seal the book, even to the time of the end: many shall run to and fro, and knowledge shall be increased." Daniel 12:4

"...but the people that do know their God shall be strong and do *exploits*." Daniel 11:32.

The manifestation of the glory of God has appeared throughout the Bible. Accounts of God's light shining on the countenance of men and women who were filled with His power to minister to the masses has been recorded throughout church history.

We see the account of Moses in Exodus 34. "And it came to pass, when Moses came down from mount Sinai with the two tables of testimony in Moses' hand, when he came down from the mount, that Moses wist not that the skin of his face shone while he talked with him." "And when Aaron and all the children of Israel saw Moses, behold, the skin of his face shone; and they were afraid to come nigh him." Exodus 34:29-30

In the Book of Acts, we see the account of Stephen's discourse when his face was like that of an angel. "And all that sat in the council, looking steadfastly on him, saw his face as it had been the face of an angel." Acts 6:15

Angels generally make appearances in the light of God's glory. They are sometimes referenced as angels of light.

As a young man I experienced an encounter with the Lord when His angel came into my bedroom during the night and the room was filled with the light of God's glory.

I have been privy to countless studies and attended church services wherein the person ministering, suddenly, was shining with the glory of God.

I was told on one occasion that the glory of God was on my face. I was only conscious of the awesome presence of the Lord at the time, so I did not know my face was shining.

After leaving a study in my youth I stopped at a convenience store. I went in to make a purchase and the people in the store gazed at me with a look as though they were seeing someone from another world. I was conscious of the presence of the Lord, but I am sure the people in the convenience store saw the glory of God.

Many congregations, while worshipping, have seen the cloud of God's glory roll into their sanctuary. These are signs of Jesus divinely and, supernaturally, walking in the midst of His people, as seen in the vision by John in Chapter 1 of Revelation, when Jesus walked in the midst of the seven golden candle sticks that represented His Church. Revelation 1:13-14

For Jesus said in Matthew 5:14 "You are the light of the world. A city that is set on a hill cannot be hidden." The words spoken by Jesus confirms forever that He is that light within us and upon us, for we have this treasure in earthen vessels. You see, we are the temple of God, we are His habitation and God is light, and in Him there is no darkness at all.

This is an awakening generation, and we are being gloriously transformed and transfigured by the glory of the Father that has come to dwell within us. We are His living stones, and we are His dwelling place. He is dwelling in our midst spiritually during this church age, but when the transfiguration is complete, we will have glorified bodies. There is also coming, a new heaven, a new earth, and a New Jerusalem where there will be no need for the sun or moon because God Himself will illuminate all with His glory.

So, let those who are born of God present their bodies unto Him in this hour and let the Holy Spirit manifest the risen Savior in these earthly vessels. There must be an awakening to the pureness of His love. See Romans 5:5b. The pureness of the love of the Father will bring a purification, followed by fresh waves of glory, releasing the power of heaven into the nations until this gospel has been preached in all the earth.

This Gospel is spanning the globe and will draw the nations to the very seat of His Throne. Many will drink of the living water and will be made new creations and give their lives to Jesus. They will have a new name that will be given them by the Lord of the harvest.

The prophet Joel spoke of the latter and former rain coming on the earth and Joel spoke of bright clouds of glory. We are seeing the glory of God in its infancy stages. As the gifts given by Jesus to men continue to mature, so will the Church. When Jesus ascended on high as Ephesians 4 declares, He gave gifts onto men.

He gave some apostles, some prophets, some evangelists, pastors, and teachers for the work of the ministry for the edification of the body and for the perfecting of the saints.

What a glorious plan of God to send His only begotten son, Jesus Christ, to become a member of fallen humanity. His death on the cross paved the way so that we could be reunited with deity.

The angels appeared on that Holy night of His birth and declared the arrival of the KING, the Messiah --the Prince of Peace --the sin substitute! Jesus was the only one found worthy in heaven or on earth who could loose the seals of the book and open heaven up to earth. See Revelation 5.

The revelation and mysteries of heaven have been released on earth through Christ our Passover. We have been granted the mystery of Christ in us, the hope of glory.

"To whom God would make known what is the riches of the glory of this mystery among the Gentiles; which is Christ in you, the hope of glory:" Colossians 1:27

God dwelt among Israel in the Old Testament, but God dwells in us in the New Covenant. We are His temple!

"And what agreement hath the temple of God with idols? for ye are the temple of the living God; as God hath said, I will dwell in them, and walk in them; and I will be their God, and they shall be my people." 2 Corinthians 6:16

In Jesus is the fullness of the Godhead bodily and those who have received Jesus as Savior have received of His fullness. Spiritually, we are completely in Him *and* we are complete in Him. Jesus lives for us, in us and through us. He was sent to the earth to rescue us so that we could be transformed and transfigured into the family of God. He is the first born of many brethren.

Isaiah declared who shall believe the report of the Lord! See Isaiah 53:1 "Who hath believed our report? and to whom is the arm of the Lord revealed?" It was reported that Jesus came in the volume of the book. It was written of Him, sacrifice thou would not, the psalmist said, but a body thou hast prepared for me. Jesus declared from the foundation of the world that He would strip Himself of His eternal glory and put on humanity. He became a mere man so that the great identification with deity and humanity could be manifested in the last days!

Jesus became as we were so that we could become as He is, and now, we who are born of God are accepted in the beloved of the Father. We have received the spirit of adoption whereby we cry Abba, Father. We have been made blameless and guiltless before our Heavenly Father. We are His very offspring, because of the awful price that was paid by the Lamb of God, Jesus Christ. He has redeemed us from the prison of the dammed and has delivered us to the very Throne Room of God where we now reign in life --joint heirs together with Christ.

We have received an incorruptible inheritance and we are reigning in the God kind of life, the zoe life, with Christ our King. When God raised Jesus from the dead there was a new creation brought forth that will continue to manifest in the earth until all things are made new.

Prayer
Father we thank you for drawing us by your love and kindness into your wonderful salvation through Christ! Let your Spirit of wisdom and revelation continue to enlighten our hearts so that the eyes of our understanding will be opened concerning the transfiguration of your Church. Lead us individually and collectively that we may reach the levels of growth and maturity needed for Christ to be glorified greatly in our mortal bodies! So, shall it be, in Jesus' name, Amen!

Highlights

1. When Christ ascended to His seated position at the right hand of the Father, He gave gifts unto men. These gifts, as noted in the following scriptures, are being used by the Lord God to bring the Church, which is His body, into full maturity. See Ephesians 4:8-13

2. Note that the ministry gifts are ordained by God, only, and not men nor the religious institutions of men. God Himself, in every generation, has and will continue to raise up ministry gifts that will take the Church to new levels of grace and glory to reach the maturity set for the generation at hand, until the Church reaches rapture-ready perfection. The readiness is based on the finished work of Christ and His being the head over all things to the Church. See Ephesians 1:22

3. So, there will be a massive revival or in gathering of new creatures, men, women, boys, and girls being born again because of the great outpouring of the latter and the former rain by the Spirit of God. Joel 2:23, Hosea 6:3. This great harvest of souls is a part of the great transfiguration and maturing of the Church. It is the mature Church that will be used to harvest this massive precious fruit of the earth in this final hour.

Reflection & Discussion Questions

1. What did God reveal to Peter, James, and John about Jesus on the mount of transfiguration?

2. What is the goal of the ministry gifts concerning the Church?

3. What is the purpose of the temple of God in the New Testament and where is it located?

Chapter 2

The Mystery Revealed

The Word of God declares the divine infinite manifold wisdom of God in 1 Corinthians, Chapter 2 concerning the mystery of the Church that was hidden before time began. We see the following scripture written by the Apostle Paul under the inspiration of the Holy Spirit concerning God's hidden wisdom that was hidden from Satan and the fallen creation.

"No, we declare God's wisdom, a mystery that has been hidden and that God destined for our glory before time began. None of the rulers of this age understood it, for if they had, they would not have crucified the Lord of glory." 1 Corinthians 2:7-8 *New International Version*

Verse seven implies that this mystery reveals God's plan to redeem a family out of the earth. As we freely accept the finished work of Christ's sinless life, of His death, burial, and resurrection, we are born again, and we are translated into the Kingdom as children of God. God had a plan from the foundation of the world to rescue fallen creation. The plan included the Word made flesh. Jesus came as the complete sacrifice to reverse the fall that came through Adam's disobedience.

When Satan and his demonic forces drove the Jewish religious leaders and the Roman government to condemn Christ to death on the cross, he was ignorant of the supreme wisdom of God that was at work in the earth through Christ. The Word of God declares that if through the trespass of the one man (Adam), death (the fallen creation) reigned through that one man, how much more will those who receive God's abundant provision of grace (salvation through Christ) and of the gift of righteousness reign in life through the one man, Jesus Christ! See Romans 5:17

It is obvious that Satan did not understand the mystery that was to be revealed, nor the glory of God that was to come to those who received salvation through Jesus Christ; therefore, Satan would not have crucified Christ if he had known this sacrifice was to deliver creation! Further clarification of the mystery is revealed in the Book of Galatians concerning the mystery and the glory that was to follow. These Scriptures give us further light into the awesome wisdom and plan of God. The wisdom of God gave His Son to be despised, rejected, beaten, stripped naked, shamefully entreated by the Roman soldiers. He was paraded in the streets of Jerusalem, and eventually led out of the city to Golgotha where He was nailed to the cross and placed under the horrible curse of the law, being made a curse for all humanity.

This all seemed the perfect ending for Christ according to Satan's plan. But God's infinite supreme wisdom was at work in that He sent His Son Jesus to ransom creation and all who would receive Jesus as Savior and Lord. See John 3:16

Death had never lost a captive and Satan was sure this would end the reign of terror he and his cohorts experienced while Jesus walked the streets of the cities of Israel. Jesus demonstrated, as a man anointed of God, divine authority and dominion over all the works of darkness for over three years. At the end of His ministry on earth He became obedient to the sufferings He had to endure for us. Christ Jesus endured all the harshness for the joy that was set before him. He endured the fullness of the curse as noted in the scripture below.

"Christ hath redeemed us from the curse of the law, being made a curse for us: for it is written, Cursed is every one that hangeth on a tree:" Galatians 3:13

The curse Jesus bore was for all humanity because all of humanity was dead and pronounced guilty before the law of the commandments that had been given through the ministry of Moses. "For all have sinned, and come short of the glory of God;" Romans 3:23.

So, all of creation and all of humanity was under the curse of this fallen creation because of Adam's transgression, but through the Old Covenant Israel had special provisions if they kept the Covenant established on Mount Sinai. The Covenant was based on the Ten Commandments and the supporting statutes and laws that were given to Moses for Israel, as noted in the upcoming verses.

"But it shall come to pass, if thou wilt not hearken unto the voice of the Lord thy God, to observe to do all his commandments and his statutes which I command thee this day; that all these curses shall come upon thee, and overtake thee:" Deuteronomy 28:15

The ministry of Moses, the law giver, is referred to as the ministry of death because when the commandments came sin revived and all were confirmed spiritually dead under the law. It is the Ten Commandments that were given by God which identifies the fallen nature of humanity. All the "thou shalt nots" identify the perverse nature of fallen man that is in direct contradiction to the nature of God.

We were never and will never be able to keep the law with the fallen nature that was passed on to all humanity by Adam. When Adam disobeyed God in the garden, he received the same awful nature Satan had inherited when he rebelled against God in Heaven.

So, God set up the Levitical priesthood which gave Israel a way to cover their sins with the sacrificial blood of animals, until the time of the final sacrifice that was to come through Jesus Christ at the end of the Old Covenant. As noted in the verses below we see God calling Aaron into the Old Covenant Priesthood.

"And thou shalt bring Aaron and his sons unto the door of the tabernacle of the congregation and wash them with water. And thou shalt put upon Aaron the holy garments, and anoint him, and sanctify him; that he may minister unto me in the priest's office. And thou shalt bring his sons, and clothe them with coats: And thou shalt anoint them, as thou didst anoint their father, that they may minister unto me in the priest's office: for their anointing shall surely be an everlasting priesthood throughout their generations." Exodus 40:12-15

"An altar of earth thou shalt make unto me, and shalt sacrifice thereon thy burnt offerings, and thy peace offerings, thy sheep, and thine oxen: in all places where I record my name I will come unto thee, and I will bless thee." Exodus 20:24

So, the priesthood was given unto the children of Israel. This priesthood was to offer animal blood sacrifices to God to cover the sins of the people. The sacrifices continued because there had to be blood shed on the altar to cover the sins. The blood of animals atoned for the sins allowed God access into Israel on a level whereby He could bless them and protect them from their enemies. Once a year the priest sacrificed a scapegoat for the sins of the people and the whole nation.

The priest pronounced the sins of Israel over the goat and released it into the wilderness so that the curse would fall in the wilderness and not on Israel, so again, we see the shadow and type of Christ depicted in the priesthood and the sacrifices of the Old Testament.

We see throughout the Old Testament individual sacrifices offered and collective offerings intended for the entire nation of Israel. Thus, all have sinned and fallen short of the glory of God. No man, except Jesus, was able to stand in the mirror of the law of the commandments without spot or blemish.

So, all of Israel, until Jesus the spotless Lamb came to atone the sins of the people, the animal sin offerings had to be made because all were sinners. Also, all nations (Gentiles) were strangers to the Covenant of promise that God established with Israel, and they were under the curse of a fallen creation. We were totally condemned to an eternal place of separation from God, to be cast into the lake of fire with all the enemies of God. This place called hell and the lake of fire was created for rebellious Satan and all his angels that followed his pride. All those that reject the new and living way given by Jesus our Lord and Savior will have to suffer the same fate.

Satan, (f/k/a) Lucifer before his rebellion, was created with awesome beauty and was filled with instruments that were fashioned to bring a melody in heaven. That melody in Lucifer led all of heaven into awesome worship and into the depths of the presence of the Most-High God! Satan and one third of the angels rebelled against God. They were condemned and placed in chains of darkness. Now Satan is a fallen evil genius going throughout the whole earth to deceive the people – the nations. He has blinded the hearts of humanity and he seeks to keep them as his slaves to continue on the earth in sin, until physical death. The verses below give an account of Satan's fall.

"How you are fallen from heaven, O Lucifer, son of the morning! How you are cut down to the ground—mighty though you were against the nations of the world. For you said to yourself, "I will ascend to heaven and rule the angels. I will take the highest throne. I will preside on the Mount of Assembly far away in the north.* I will climb to the highest heavens and be like the Most High." But instead, you will be brought down to the pit of hell, down to its lowest depths. Everyone there will stare at you and ask, "Can this be the one who shook the earth and the kingdoms of the world? Can this be the one who destroyed the world and made it into a shambles, who demolished its greatest cities and had no mercy on his prisoners?" Isaiah 14:12-17, *The Living Bible*

So, Satan was cast out of heaven like lighting, and the Scripture declared a warning to the inhabitants of the earth as noted below:

"Therefore rejoice, ye heavens, and ye that dwell in them. Woe to the inhabiters of the earth and of the sea! for the devil is come down unto you, having great wrath, because he knoweth that he hath but a short time." Revelation 12:12, *21st Century King James Version*

So, Satan subverted the authority Adam had been given by God and became the god of this world. Satan deceived and tricked his way into gaining the authority Adam had been given by the Lord in the of Eden, as noted in Genesis, Chapter 3 below:

"Now the serpent was more subtil than any beast of the field which the Lord God had made. And he said unto the woman, Yea, hath God said, Ye shall not eat of every tree of the garden? And the woman said unto the serpent, We may eat of the fruit of the trees of the garden: But of the fruit of the tree which is in the midst of the garden, God hath said, Ye shall not eat of it, neither shall ye touch it, lest ye die. And the serpent said unto the woman, Ye shall not surely die: For God doth know that in the day ye eat thereof, then your eyes shall be opened, and ye shall be as gods, knowing good and evil. And when the woman saw that the tree was good for food, and that it was pleasant to the eyes, and a tree to be desired to make one wise, she took of the fruit thereof, and did eat, and gave also unto her husband with her; and he did eat. And the eyes of them both were opened, and they knew that they were naked; and they sewed fig leaves together and made themselves aprons." Genesis 3:1 – 7

After Adam's fall God's wisdom and plan of redemption for man was to send Jesus, born of a virgin --fully God and fully man --to offer Himself once and for all a sacrifice for sin. See Isaiah 7:14 The Holy Spirit overshadowed Mary and she was with child. Because of this Immaculate Conception, Mary brought forth a Son who is the new and living way, who has bridged heaven and earth. (See, Luke 1:31) What a glorious mystery and truth! The Word of God made flesh to dwell among men! See John 1:14 But the enemy, Satan, understood not the mystery that was to ensue because of the birth of Jesus and His death on the cross, or he would not have crucified the Lamb of God. The wisdom of God was to allow Jesus, who knew no sin, to become sin for us. Once Jesus took our sin in His body, He was then ready to take all our punishment. The punishment was not only the many stripes 39 times that represented the 39 categories of diseases, but the chastisement of our peace (mental anguish and mental illness). Every spiritual, physical, and emotional curse that could be encountered on the earth by humanity was placed on Jesus.

The ultimate suffering ensued when Jesus died spiritually. The spiritual death opened the door to physical death. It is no wonder Jesus cried out on the cross, "My God, My God, why hast thou forsaken me?" Matthew 27:46b. You see, for Jesus to finish the work of redemption He had to descend, down into hell. And for three days and three nights He suffered God's full wrath for us by taking all that the forces of darkness could inflict upon Him. All that the fullness of humanity was destined to suffer in hell Jesus suffered until the claims of God's court of justice were satisfied. We see in the Scriptures below the awful price Jesus paid.

"Surely He has borne our griefs (sicknesses, weaknesses, and distresses) and carried our sorrows and pains [of punishment], yet we [ignorantly] considered Him stricken, smitten, and afflicted by God [as if with leprosy]. But He was wounded for our transgressions, He was bruised for our guilt and iniquities; the chastisement [needful to obtain] peace and well-being for us was upon Him, and with the stripes [that wounded] Him we are healed and made whole. All we like sheep have gone astray, we have turned every one to his own way; and the Lord has made to light upon Him the guilt and iniquity of us all. He was oppressed, [yet when] He was afflicted, He was submissive and opened not His mouth; like a lamb that is led to the slaughter, and as a sheep before her shearers is dumb, so He opened not His mouth. By oppression and judgment He was taken away; and as for His generation, who among them considered that He was cut off out of the land of the living [stricken to His death] for the transgression of my [Isaiah's] people, to whom the stroke was due?" Isaiah 53:4-8, *Amplified Bible Classic Edition*

"Just as there were many who were appalled at him his appearance was so disfigured beyond that of any human being and his form marred beyond human likeness— so he will sprinkle many nations, and kings will shut their mouths because of him. For what they were not told, they will see, and what they have not heard, they will understand."
Isaiah 52:14-15 *New International Version*

The suffering of Jesus went far beyond the cross on Calvary. After His physical death He descended into the lowest bowels of hell. There in hell he paid a price we cannot imagine, and all the tormentors of darkness converged on Him to bring the worst that can be offered in sufferings in any realm. See Psalm 22

Once justice was served the glory of the Father descended down into hell and fulfilled the Holy Scriptures. The psalmist wrote that God would not leave His (Jesus') soul in hell nor would God suffer His Holy One to see corruption. In other words, His body would not see what all humanity had seen in physical death. See Psalm 16:10

Before death could start the decomposition of His body, the resurrection power of God surged through the Spirit of the Lamb and brought Him up out of hell with total victory over death. Jesus went back into His body and there was a phenomenon that occurred that would change the laws of the universe, forever. Matthew gave the following account of the death and resurrection of Jesus.

"At that moment, the curtain in the sanctuary of the Temple was torn in two, from top to bottom. The earth shook, rocks split apart, and tombs opened. The bodies of many godly men and women who had died were raised from the dead. They left the cemetery after Jesus' resurrection, went into the holy city of Jerusalem, and appeared to many people."
Matthew 27:51-53 *New Living Translation*

It was the glorious resurrection power of God that changed what was earthly into that which is spiritual and heavenly. It was the Lamb being clothed with the priestly garment of a resurrected body so that He could enter the Holy of Holies, with His own blood and take His place as our High Priest at the right hand of the Father where He ever maketh intercession for us. He died for us! He rose for us! He lives for us! He lives in us! We have been raised spiritually, together with Him, to reign and rule with Him, forever.

Jesus is the first born of many brethren. When Jesus became sin for us, He died spiritually and was separated from the Father so that He could pay the full price for our sins. So, when Jesus became sin and ascended into Hades, He was separated from the Father. He died both spiritually and physically. He suffered as the Son of Man in Hades. After the claims of God's justice was satisfied by the Lamb's supreme sacrifice, God announced that Jesus was now a Son again unto Himself, and He God, was again a Father unto Him (Jesus)! See Psalm 2:7 and Hebrews 1:5

The zoe (God life) of God surged into the regions of hell and raised Jesus up a new creation, setting the stage for the recreation of all things! When Jesus died, we died with Him and when Jesus was raised from the dead, we were raised up together with Him. The Word declares "Therefore we are buried with him by baptism into death: that like as Christ was raised up from the dead by the glory of the Father, even so we also should walk in newness of life." Romans 6:4. Glory to God! We have been filled with the very life that is in God the Father. God, through the person of the Holy Spirit, has come to abide with us forever because of the blood of the Lamb.

Paul, under the inspiration of the Holy Spirit, declared that it is Christ in you (us), the hope of glory. We are one spirit with the Lord. We are vessels of honor because Christ is the treasure that fills our vessels, even with His eternal life. We have this treasure in earthen vessels that the excellency of the power may be of God and not of ourselves. See 2 Corinthians 4:7

It is God who has brought forth the mystery of creation in our hearts. God, through the finished work of Christ, took fallen humanity and elevated him beyond his original state before the fall. Adam had lost the beauty and glory of God that was upon him, but after the fall, Adam gave that dominion and authority over to Satan. When Adam and Eve partook of the forbidden tree they yielded to the counsel of Satan and took on his nature. So, Satan became the god of this world and brought death and sorrow to humanity. Corruption and pure evil were found in man after the fall, and so great was the fall that God allowed a flood to destroy all but Noah and the souls who were shut up in the ark.

God promised Noah there would be no more flooding of the whole earth. God was now setting the stage to establish a Covenant that would give Him legal and divine access back into the earth to reconcile all that would receive reconciliation.

God's plan of reconciliation took humanity way beyond the place from which Adam fell. After the death, burial, and resurrection of Jesus, a door was opened into Heaven to welcome in the family of God. The Scripture declares in 1 Corinthians, Chapter 15 that the first man, Adam, was of this earth and was created a living soul but the second Adam, Jesus Christ, was created a spiritual body. So, God no longer had to visit man in the cool of the garden in his earthly domain, but God Himself, by the finished work of Jesus Christ, has raised us up together with Him which enabled us to be seated in heavenly places with Christ.

You see, we are His dwelling place; we are His living stones; and with Jesus Christ being the chief corner stone, we are built up together as a habitation of the Lord, in Him! God always does exceedingly abundantly above all that we ask or think. See Ephesians 2:20-22

He has prepared an eternal city for us built with His own hands and fashioned with His own eternal creative powers. "But as it is written, Eye hath not seen, nor ear heard, neither have entered into the heart of man, the things which God hath prepared for them that love him", (See 1 Corinthians 2:9-10a) but He has revealed them unto us by His Spirit!

His salvation includes the best of this world and the world to come. The scripture says in 1 Timothy 4:8 "For bodily exercise profits a little, but godliness is profitable for all things, having promise of the life that now is and of that which is to come." The Lord has made us rich, and He adds no sorrow with it. He delights in the prosperity of His people. He (anyone) who will give their life to Christ will gain eternal life right here on earth, which entitles us to all the resources and wealth here on earth and in Heaven. The Apostle Paul said all things are yours! Jesus said seek ye first the Kingdom of God and His righteousness and all these things will be added unto you. We do not have to sweat and toil.

We are no longer alienated from the life of God, and we can now partake of His divine nature. Beloved, John said under the inspiration of the Holy Spirit, I wish above all things that you may prosper and be in health even as your soul prospers. God has made us masters over all the works of darkness.

He has called us more than conquerors. He has called us kings and priests unto Himself. He has called us sons, of the Most-High God. The angels stand in awe of the wonderful work of God in us for they see He has crowned us and given us Sonship. We are crowned with our Heavenly Father's love and kindness. By His grace, we have set our affection on things above and our conversation is in Heaven with our Father.

We have been made the righteousness of God by the finished work of Jesus. We have fellowship with the Father when we allow our recreated human spirits to govern our lives and when we commune with Him. Christians who remain in carnality will never know the true blessing and reality of this new life in the Father while they live here on the earth.
We must commit ourselves unto the Word of the Lord and the tender love of the Father.

The Epistles written to the Church are the foundation of the apostles ordained and commissioned of God by the Holy Spirit. The Epistles are His love letters to the Church, His bride.

God has ordained that we feed on the sincere milk of His Word that we may grow there by. We can never enjoy the meat of God's Word until we have had enough milk to develop spiritual teeth. Once we develop spiritual teeth we can feast at the table of God and enjoy the heavenly banquet spread before us. No good thing has He withheld from His children. He has given us all things freely to enjoy. He has blessed us with all spiritual blessings in heavenly places. If we have the blessings of Heaven, then it is certain we will have His blessings here on earth. The Word of God declares thy will be done in earth, as it is in Heaven.

Baby Christians and carnal Christians are self-conscious. They are ruled by their physical senses. They are tuned into the voices of this world. They are infatuated with the world and have not fully grasped the Word as declared in 1 John 2:15-16: "Love not the world, neither the things that are in the world. If any man loves the world, the love of the Father is not in him. For all that is in the world, the lust of the flesh, and the lust of the eyes, and the pride of life, is not of the Father, but is of the world." Carnal Christians are easily distracted and ruled by their physical senses. They are emotionally driven and easily offended, which is why the Spirit of God spoke through the Apostle Paul and warned that novice should not be placed in leadership positions in the church. They are susceptible to pride and self-importance. They are tossed to and fro, by every wind of doctrine by the cunning of men.

The only way to grow spiritually is to have a constant steady diet of the Word of God, specifically the New Testament, because this is where mystery is revealed. We are told in the New Testament Epistles who Christ is in us and who we are in Christ. The New Testament also teaches us what we have in Christ. We have been given authority, power, and dominion in Christ. We have been granted access to come boldly to the Throne of grace to receive help. We are the manifested Sons of God revealed in these last days. We have been reunited with the divine authority that was lost in the Garden of Eden, but that authority now dwells within us (God dwells in us). We are reigning with Christ Jesus! See Romans 5:17

We have been given His Spirit and we are sealed by His Spirit until the redemption of our bodies is made manifest. We are the Church of the living God, the pillow and ground of the truth. We are His workmanship. We are the salt of the earth, a city on a hill that cannot be hid. Spiritually, we have come unto mount Zion, unto New Jerusalem, unto an innumerable company of angels, unto the general assembly and Church of the firstborn which are written in Heaven and to God, the Judge of all, unto the spirits of just men made perfect. See Hebrews 12:22-24

All these wonderful truths are found in the Epistles, and they are included in the mystery revealed to us in these last days. We have glorious access to Heaven as children of God. The Old Testament is relevant only as we see it, in light of the New Testament, and through the eyes of our hearts that we are born of God. Then we can see the shadows and types of the new creation and kingdom that has come in the writings of the old and new!

When Jesus was raised from the dead, He met two disciples on the road to Emmaus. Jesus began to open the Scriptures of the prophets of the Old Testament and revealed to them the very plan of God which included the sufferings of Jesus in His death, burial, and resurrection.

Their hearts burned in them as they were taught by the risen Savior. The joy of the Lord began to strengthen and comfort their souls. The despair and pain of the Savior's death was lifted, and their eyes were completely opened as Jesus sat and brake bread with them. What jubilation must have filled their hearts as they journeyed back to Jerusalem to share this exciting news with the other disciples!

So again, it is the New Testament that has placed us in Christ, and it is the perfect law of liberty that has given us life. We are transformed into the very image of God from glory to glory as we feast on the Word of the living God. No, it is not the intellect of our minds, but it is the revelation of light and Truth taught by the Spirit of Truth. God has anointed believers to preach and teach under the power of His new life. Every believer is anointed to hear what the Spirit is saying to the Church. It is the anointing or unction; you could also say the Spirit of God teaches us all things because they are all synonymous terms. The scriptures below give us light on how we are taught by God's anointing/unction.

"But ye have an unction from the Holy One, and ye know all things." But the anointing which ye have received of him abideth in you, and ye need not that any man teach you: but as the same anointing teacheth you of all things, and is truth, and is no lie, and even as it hath taught you, ye shall abide in him." (1 John 2:20, 27) This means we must be anointed to hear, and the teacher or preacher must be called, anointed, and sent by God if they are to teach God's people the mysteries of the Kingdom. It is quite obvious many have taken it upon themselves to minister to God's people, but they were never called of God, and others who were called of God never took the time to get before qualified anointed men and women to be taught by the Holy Spirit.

God is raising up an army in this last hour that will walk in the light of this mystery of Christ in humility. This army will not be tainted by religion, humanism, nor the secularism of this age. They will go forth in the reality of the Kingdom of Christ. Some are not of this army and march in error, they have not become disciples of Truth. A leader can be right in their heart (born of God) but in error in their head or doctrine if they have not been taught to walk in the light of God's Truth. It is God who places members in the body, and He knows where we belong. We need to be a part of a local church where truth is taught so that we can grow and serve in the body of Christ. It cannot be overstated how important it is to allow God to give us pastors after His own heart.

There are those walking in the light of this great mystery that has been revealed concerning God's plan from the beginning, even from the foundation of the world, that we would be found in Christ and in His glory in this Church age. Jesus was slain from the foundation of the world and revealed in these last days. The power that was wrought in Christ when He was raised from the dead is still in operation throughout the earth and will be until the New Heaven and New Earth have come into full manifestation and the city that has been prepared like a bride for her husband will come to the New Earth. God's Throne will be in the center of that city!

34

Prayer

Father, thank you for the mystery of Christ in us, the hope of glory. Thank you, Jesus, for your supreme sacrifice that has brought us into Sonship. Father we continue to yield to you freely that we may grow into the mature elect that you have called us unto in these last days. We present our bodies a living sacrifice unto you freely. For there is no other place to be compared with than being in the center of your love and plan. Thank you for your wonderful salvation and redemption! In Jesus' name we pray, Amen!

Highlights

1. When Satan and his demonic forces drove the Jewish leaders and the Roman government to condemn Christ to death on the cross, he was ignorant of the supreme wisdom of God that was at work in the earth through Christ. The Word of God declares that if through the trespass of the one man (Adam), death (the fallen creation) reigned through that one man, how much more will those who receive God's abundant provision of grace (salvation through Christ) and of the gift of righteousness reign in life through the one man, Jesus Christ! Romans 5:17

2. Christ has redeemed us from the curse of the fallen creation and has reunited us with the Father as His dear children. We are now the children of God.

3. His salvation includes the best of this world and the world to come. The scripture says in 1 Timothy 4:8 that godliness is profitable unto all things having promise of the life that now is and that which is to come. The Lord has made us rich, and He adds no sorrow with it. He delights in the prosperity of His people.

Reflection & Discussion Questions

1. What happened to creation, as a result of Adam's disobedience, and what happened to the authority that Adam was given, in the Garden of Eden?

2. What is the purpose of the Ten Commandments and is it possible to keep the Ten Commandments today and receive salvation without Christ Jesus?

3. As born-again believers in Christ, can we expect to have any level of authority over Satan? If so, why should a believer expect to have any authority?

4. What is God's plan for this fallen creation?

Chapter 3

Established in Christ

We have been established in Christ as Kingdom heirs and heirs of God. We are established as joint heirs together with Christ. We are baptized into Christ Jesus and have been baptized into His Name. Christ is to the Church (His body) what the husband is to be to his wife in Holy matrimony. The wife takes on the husband's name. Lovingly and legally the wife becomes one with her husband, sharing his name and all his possessions.

In a real commitment to one another a man and a woman before God are joined together, becoming one flesh. This is a Holy and sacred union that is treasured as the two become one and the marriage is sealed with the joy of consummation. The marriage, if lived in the New Covenant light of the Father, will reflect Christ and the Church. The husband is to love, nurture and tenderly care for his wife as Christ does for His bride, the Church. As the Lord Jesus gave Himself for the Church through His supreme sacrifice, it was so that we the Church could be eternally established in Him who is our loving Savior, forever.

We are to have a divine, Holy love feast with Christ, that not only establishes us in Him but also transfigures us with His glory. This transfiguration is to continue until we, the Church, here on the earth reach full zenith in His likeness. When we have reached the fullness of the measure of the stature of Christ, we will be changed in a moment --in the twinkling of an eye. We will be raptured and caught up with Christ from the old creation, forever. What is the reason for this great establishment in Christ and constant transfiguration? It is the answer to the call of creation that has been groaning and waiting for the manifested sons of God to appear on the earth. Creation has been waiting for the mature, elect, and established children of God who would manifest the glory of God (the power of God) on the earth. The earth has been waiting since the fall when Adam gave away the glory he had in the garden through disobedience. The elect, mature, and established ones in Christ are the instruments of the Lord to bring about His will in these last days before the return of Christ. We are kings and priests unto God. We are stewards of the Gospel of Jesus Christ. We are a Holy nation and a peculiar people. We are living stones, and Jesus Christ, being the chief corner stone. We are built together in Christ to be the living temple of God. Because of this divine establishment, we are to walk in the authority and dominion at levels that have not been seen since Christ walked the earth.

We are to do the works of Christ and greater works than He did. There is to be a progressive increase in the manifestation of the glory of God in the earth. The manifestation should be occurring as a result of the increased intimacy the Church is having with Christ.

This intimacy with Christ will cause the earth to be filled with the knowledge and the glory of the Lord! This increase in knowledge will result in the sowing of the seed of the Word, bringing a gentle rain upon the nations. This is the latter and former rain spoken of by the prophet concerning the Word of God to the nations. The technology and social media of the day is lending itself to the propagation (or spreading) of the Word of God, moving humanity from a dead Christless religion that is void of the wonderful compassion of the Lord Jesus.

The Word of God is flowing from nations where God has taken men into an Apostolic anointing so the mysteries concerning Christ and the Church can be made known in deeper dimentions. The revelation of Jesus Christ is our sure foundation that we are established in, built up in Him, who is the living Word. He is the Rock that we also build on as opposed to the religious sinking sand that has plagued a great many of the evangelical world in this country who have erred from the true faith of our Lord, causing many to become stranded in social ideology.

We see a large movement of the so-called evangelicals who have come into alignment with political and social agendas. As a result, men's hearts have left the compassion for Christ. Some believers have adopted a platform driven by social privileges to preserve political power and influential gain, as opposed to remaining rooted and grounded in the love of God. We see many turning to the secular, political, cultural, and philosophical whelms that were designed by darkness to desensitize the Church and cause believers to lose sight of the reality of the true teachings (The Gospel) of Christ. But the gates of hell will not prevail against this Church of Jesus Christ. God will cause salvation to flourish in the earth in this hour from every tongue and every kindred upon the earth.

God the Father will continue to purge leadership at every level. The scripture speaks of the pulling down of strongholds, casting down imaginations and every high thing that will attempt to exalt itself above the knowledge and plan of the Lord. See 2 Corinthians 10:4-5

This work will not be done by the wisdom and ideas of men. The work will not be done through a people who have lost sight of the resurrection power that raised Jesus from the dead. The works will not be done by those who rely on politics and the laws that govern nations on the earth. You can appoint conservative judges to the Supreme Court; you can reverse Roe vs. Wade; or you can attempt to control this fallen creation by any carnal means necessary through laws and legislation. Sure, we should pray and ask God to raise up men and women in every sphere of influence, whether it be in governing or any other discipline. Yes, we should vote and participate in the political process, but these things must be done in God's love, and they must not have fleshly and selfish agendas.

You cannot legislate the hearts of men. After all the efforts of men without the Lord, including efforts that are void of the unconditional love, power, and salvation of the Lord Jesus Christ, it is for nothing. The Scripture declares that unless the Lord builds the house, they labor in vain that build it. Whether it be a city, nation, learning institution, government, businesses, or household, if the Lord is not in the structuring, it counts for nothing. Without God's love we are noisy brass and tinkling cymbals. What we do has to be --it must be established in Christ and His love if it is to transfer into eternity! We must operate in the established wisdom from above, from the very Throne of God. God's wisdom is pure, peaceable, easily entreated, full of good fruits, without partiality and without hypocrisy!

A vast majority of those who call themselves the Church have drifted into religion and legalism. They have fallen into the subtle deception of the prince of this world (Satan).

Those who have rallied behind an administration that is spewing hate, racism and division have either lost sight of Christ or they never knew Him! Jesus said they will know you are my disciples by your love. The Word says we know we have passed from death unto life because we love our brothers (the Church and humanity).

39

The Word says he that hates his brother is a murderer. The Word of God says how can you say you have the love of God in your heart if you see your brother in need and refuse him help. We are also told to love our neighbors as ourselves. Jesus told the following parable, explaining how we should respond to a neighbor. One of the Jews asked Jesus "...And who is my neighbor?" and Jesus responded with the following parable:

In reply Jesus said: "A man was going down from Jerusalem to Jericho, when he was attacked by robbers. They stripped him of his clothes, beat him and went away, leaving him half dead. A priest happened to be going down the same road, and when he saw the man, he passed by on the other side. So too, a Levite, when he came to the place and saw him, passed by on the other side. But a Samaritan, as he traveled, came where the man was; and when he saw him, he took pity on him. He went to him and bandaged his wounds, pouring on oil and wine. Then he put the man on his own donkey, brought him to an inn and took care of him. The next day he took out two denarii and gave them to the innkeeper. 'Look after him,' he said, 'and when I return, I will reimburse you for any extra expense you may have.' "Which of these three do you think was a neighbor to the man who fell into the hands of robbers?'" Luke 10:30-36 *New International Version*

We can determine from this parable that humanity, around the globe, is our neighbor. Wherever there is darkness, injustice, poverty, sickness and/or civil unrest, we are to allow the grace of our Lord to equip us to help!

In this nation we have seen, in recent times, leaders who were called and anointed of God turn from their calling and devote much time and effort supporting hate and division under the assumption that they were being led of God. True children of God who are walking in the love of God are out to bless humanity, not curse or divide it. The Scripture says we are the seed of Abraham, so in Christ the seed and the whole earth is to be blessed by us --not abused! The Word says the love of God in us does not rejoice in injustice, nor unrighteousness, but rejoices in Truth and that which is right (justice). "It does not rejoice at injustice and unrighteousness, but rejoices when right and truth prevail." 1 Corinthians 13:6, *Amplified Bible Classic Edition*

God's Word says he that walks with wise men shall be wise but those who walk with evil men will be destroyed. (See Proverbs 13:20) If a man is constantly lying and pushing hate, any Christian who supports the evildoers are promoting evil. These supporters are enablers, and they are sowing to the flesh seeds of destruction which will be reaped. They have left the first love of Christ and are now in danger of His judgment. Any group that promotes anything outside of the love of God is in the control of satanic darkness. They are slaves of darkness and are potentially headed for eternal punishment.

The works of Christ will not be done by those who have submerged themselves in politics. Nor will the works be done by simple theology and religion on purely an intellectual level. There are many who were never born of God, or called of God and yet ventured into religion, which is man's quest to find and please God by his own works. Christianity is man's response and reception of the finished work of Christ, knowing that Jesus is the spotless Lamb who paid the full price for the salvation of the whole world.

The work of God will not be done by selfish self-righteous sectarianism. This work will be done by those having the end of their faith in Jesus Christ who is the same yesterday today and forever! The work will be done in and by those who have received the great commission, which was spoken by Jesus before His ascension. He said go ye into all the world and preach the Gospel! This Gospel is the Good News and glad tidings of peace. Jesus said come unto me all you who are weighted down or burdened, and I will give you salvation and rest. Those who are the mature, elect and established in Christ will teach and preach the pureness of the Gospel. These mature ones will go forth with the Holy Spirit in the operation of the Spirit's power with signs, wonders and miracles following.

Those who depend on wit, control, manipulation, and intellectual arguments to win the lost have lost sight of the head of the Church or they never knew Him. They are preaching another Jesus and have fallen from the true grace. The Word of God says by love and kindness have I drawn you. There is a way that seems right unto men, but the end is destruction. They are trying to use carnal, fleshly means to accomplish what only the Spirit of God can do through yielded vessels on the earth.

The more intimacy we have with our Lord, His grace and peace will multiply in our lives. This multiplication of grace and peace increases the fruitfulness of His Church. The Church will travail in prayer and deed, giving birth and salvation to many throughout the nations.

This divine mandate will escalate in this hour, for God has said I will do a quick work in that day. We are being transformed and transfigured as His body here on the earth, daily. God the Father is at work in us, preparing us to receive the fullness of the manifestation of our inheritance with Jesus.

Jesus left His Throne in glory to come to the earth to rescue a people that would share His glory. I do not say that we should take His glory through fleshly and vain selfish validation. The Word declares that He (God) will not give to or share His glory with another. But for those born of God who are living out of their recreated spirits shall walk in the light of John 17:22 where Jesus declared that the glory given Him by the Father would be given unto us (believers) because we are His body.

Jesus is the seed that was sent from Heaven to the earth to birth the triumphant Church. He is the head of the Church and over all things to the Church. He is the Chief Shepard, Chief Apostle and High Priest over His Church. Jesus has many other titles, but for now, let us focus on His body, the Church, in the earth.

In Ephesians, the Scripture says we are a part of Christ's body.
"For we are members of his body, of his flesh, and of his bones."
Ephesians 5:30

This Truth gives us light concerning the oneness we have with Christ as we are members of His body, as much as or more than we are members that make up our physical bodies. In 1 Corinthians, Chapter 6 the Word of God further emphasizes this Truth referencing Christ's members.
"Know ye not that your bodies are the members of Christ?" 1 Corinthians 6:15a and verse 17 of the same Chapter declares it is the spirit within the physical body that is joined unto Christ. "But he that is joined unto the Lord is one spirit." 1 Corinthians 6:17

Our bodies are members of Christ because our spirit man is housed in our physical body. The body moves and lives because of the life in the spirit man, or the hidden man of the heart. James said the body without the spirit is dead. God's Word declares that for believers to be absent from the body is to be present with the Lord. See 2 Corinthians 5:8

In Acts 9:4, Saul, who was on his way to Damascus to persecute the Church, fell to the ground as a result of his encounter with Christ. The light of God shone brighter than the noon day sun and Saul heard a voice saying unto him, "Saul, Saul, why persecutest thou me?" Saul was persecuting believers. Jesus saw no difference between the Church (believers) and Himself because the Church is His body. So, Saul was on his way to persecute the body of Christ. These born-again believers were born of God and baptized into Christ by the Spirit of God. I am not referring to water baptism but a spiritual baptism that occurs supernaturally when we accept Jesus as Savior and Lord.

"For surely you know that when we were baptized into union with Christ Jesus, we were baptized into union with his death. By our baptism, then, we were buried with him and shared his death, in order that, just as Christ was raised from death by the glorious power of the Father, so also we might live a new life." Romans 6:3-4 *Good News Translation*

That Greek word for life is zoe which means the God kind of life, So, our dead spirit was baptized into Christ and raised up together with Him to walk in the zoe (life) of God. Jesus said I come to give you zoe (life) and zoe (life) more abundantly. Our spirits have eternal life in them now and we are living in Christ. We are members of His body.

There is a divine new birth and union that happens in the realm of the spirit that cannot be explained with the vocabularies of this world. We become one spirit with our Lord Jesus and our Heavenly Father. This is a wonderful and divine occasion orchestrated by the power of God that has brought forth a Kingdom and a new creation that will never end. Note: Our spirits live forever, either in Heaven or hell, one place or the other.

We are a new creation in Christ. See 2 Corinthians 5:17. We have been born of God and we are His children. God's Word tells us in 1 John 3:1, "Behold, what manner of love the Father hath bestowed upon us, that we should be called the sons of God:" In the Book of Romans, Chapter 8:29b, it says Jesus is the first born of many children. Jesus merited our right to this sacred union in His death, burial, and resurrection. We will be forever growing in the revelation of this glorious act of divine love and power that brought forth the reconciling of man and deity. We also see Heaven and earth passing away in an explosion of fire as referenced in 2 Peter 3:10. "But the day of the LORD will come as a thief in the night; in the which the heavens shall pass away with a great noise, and the elements shall melt with fervent heat, the earth also and the works that are therein shall be burned up." We see here that because we are reunited to God in Christ all of creation will one day be destroyed and made new. The following verses of 2 Peter 10, as recorded: "Seeing then that all these things shall be dissolved, what manner of persons ought ye to be in all holy conversation and godliness, looking for and hasting unto the coming of the day of God, wherein the heavens being on fire shall be dissolved, and the elements shall melt with fervent heat? Nevertheless we, according to his promise, look for new heavens and a new earth, wherein dwelleth righteousness." See vs. 11-13 So, we see God working to make all things new through the finished work of Jesus.

This is the very reason all of creation has been groaning and waiting for the manifestation of the Sons of God. Creation groaned to be one with the Creator. It groans to be freed from corruption so that it could put on incorruption, even as we groan in our bodies to pull off the mortal bodies and put on the immortal bodies. The dead in Christ shall rise first and we who remain on the earth shall be changed, in a moment and in the twinkling of an eye at the last trump. We are reigning on earth because we have been made brand new creatures in our spirits. In the New Testament the word spirit and heart are synonymous terms. We see the Prophet Ezekiel speaking prophetically by the Holy Spirit, declaring the new birth in our hearts (our spirits).

We find the following in Ezekiel 36:25-27: "Then will I sprinkle clean water upon you, and ye shall be clean: from all your filthiness, and from all your idols, will I cleanse you. A new heart also will I give you, and a new spirit will I put within you: and I will take away the stony heart out of your flesh, and I will give you a heart of flesh. And I will put my spirit within you, and cause you to walk in my statutes, and ye shall keep my judgments, and do them."

God declared clearly in the Scriptures that we would need a new heart. Man's heart and nature was perverted because of the fall. God was talking to Israel, His chosen people, but we will see later that because of Israel's rejection of Christ, God turned to the Gentiles with this great blessing to provoke Israel to jealousy.

God has always had a plan from the beginning, for all of humanity but He needed a man (Abraham) and a people (Israel) to give Him legal access back into the earth. God had turned the earth over to Adam and Adam turned it over to Satan when he disobeyed God in the garden. Satan became the prince of this world. God had a plan from the beginning to take back the earth and His family. "For God so loved the world that he gave his only begotten Son, that whosoever believeth in him should not perish, but have everlasting life." John 3:16

Notice that God sent Jesus for the whole world. Because of the sacrifice of Christ and His shed blood, a New Covenant, based on better promises was established. God Himself established this Covenant in the life and blood of the spotless Lamb. There were no requirements on the part of man. In the Old Covenant man could be blessed if he hearkened diligently unto the voice of the Lord and kept all the commandments given by God. But in the New Covenant God sent Jesus Christ, who solved the problem of the sins of the whole world when He died and went to hell for all humanity.

When Jesus went into the Holy of Holies after His resurrection from the dead He entered in with His own blood once and for all to declare sin wiped away for all who would receive His ransom. We see in Jeremiah 31 that God also spoke prophetically concerning this New Covenant that would come centuries in advance.

"Behold, the days come, saith the Lord, that I will make a New Covenant with the house of Israel, and with the house of Judah: "Not according to the covenant that I made with their fathers in the day that I took them by the hand to bring them out of the land of Egypt; which my covenant they brake, although I was an husband unto them, saith the Lord: But this shall be the covenant that I will make with the house of Israel; after those days, saith the Lord, I will put my law in their inward parts, and write it in their hearts; and will be their God, and they shall be my people. And they shall teach no more every man his neighbor, and every man his brother, saying, Know the Lord: for they shall all know me, from the least of them unto the greatest of them, saith the Lord: for I will forgive their iniquity, and I will remember their sin no more." Jeremiah 31:31-34

So, we have a New Covenant, with better promises, which is revealed in the writings of the New Testament. See Hebrews 8:6: "But now hath he obtained a more excellent ministry, by how much also he is the mediator of a better covenant, which was established upon better promises."

The Covenant declares Jesus, the author and finisher of our salvation and our faith. He sacrificed His life in obedience to the Father. Because of His supreme sacrifice we have a new and living way into His Kingdom. We will worship and praise Him forever and ever because only Jesus could bring us back into fellowship with the Father. Worthy is the Lamb that was slain! As many as received Him gave He grace and power to become the sons of God.

We who are born of God and have been placed in the body of Christ have taken our portion with the GREAT. God *is* that GREATNESS and there is none to compare. His greatness is larger than the universe. When we consider the vastness of the universe, we are just entering the door of understanding the infinity of the Father and His power:

Prayer
Father, we thank you that through the finished work of Christ we have been redeemed from destruction and hate. We have been translated into your Kingdom and established in Christ our Savior. We continue to present ourselves unto you so that we are no longer conformed to this world. We receive the transformation by your Truth being fully established on the foundation of Christ and Him alone! Amen!

Highlights
1. We have been baptized into Christ and joined unto the Lord as a husband is joined unto his wife in Holy matrimony.

2. We are baptized into the name of Jesus and have received a new heart and we are a new species.

3. We have received His commission to go into all the world and make disciples.

Reflection & Discussion Questions
1. What must happen in the life of a person, in order to receive the foundation to be established in Christ?

2. If a person has been established in Christ, who is their neighbor?

3. What should be the driving force in the heart of every believer and why?

Chapter 4

He Gave Gifts

Man is a spirit, he has a soul, and he lives in a body. God, the Father of spirits from the beginning, created man to be a living soul to be dominated by his spirit that was in fellowship with God. The Scripture says God is a Spirit and they that worship Him must worship Him in spirit and truth. See John 4:24. We were created in God's class because we were made in His image and likeness. See Genesis 2. After the fall of Adam and Eve in the Garden of Eden, Adam lost the wonderful fellowship he enjoyed with God, but it has been restored to us who believe in and through the finished work of Jesus Christ. The finished work of Christ is working in the earth and it is in the process of making all things new. We see the birth pains and a travailing on a global level; this is reflected by the many issues documented in the Word of God, which speaks of these end time events centuries ago.

In this hour of predicted constant global challenges, we see concerns referencing global warming, rising national/global debt, and constant disputes over international territories. There is the threat of war continuously between nations, as the Scripture says there shall be wars and rumors of wars. So, we see nations in conflict over resources and territorial disputes. Also, there is the never ending political, social, and religious differences that plague our global community. These vast and diverse issues of humanity are being addressed by fallen man, who resorts to using the only means he can forge, which are ineffective limited abilities that impact, very little, apart from God. This world, excluding the true Church of believers, is drowning in pride, selfishness and hate because the world has been blinded by the prince of this world, Satan.

Satan, through his centuries of deception, has gained strongholds over nations and peoples because they have rejected the Creator of the heavens and the earth. Because of this rejection we see that God has turned a vast portion of humanity over to strong delusions. Humanity, at large, have gone about to establish their own righteousness and every man/nation is doing what they perceive to be right in their own eyes. Even the natural use of that which God established in pro creation has been changed and perverted by a fallen creation. This is not an indictment, nor a condemnation but rather an assessment and observation, in light of God's original plan and purpose for humanity.

God loves fallen humanity! "For God so loved the world that He gave His only begotten son that whosoever believeth in Him should not perish but have everlasting life." John 3:16.

God the Creator, through the mouth of His Son, has declared He is not out to condemn the world because the world is already condemned. He is out to reconcile man unto Himself through the supreme sacrifice of Christ. He said if any man will come unto me I will in no wise cast him out! God hates sin so He sent His Son of Love to die for the sinners! The true Church does not hate the sinners, nor does it condemn the sinners, but rather, is reaching out with loving arms to all humanity to say Jesus loves you and I do too! This Church not only has the answer for lost humanities' spiritual death, but it has the answer to the soul of the nations. God's wisdom and power is poised to address every diverse issue on the planet. God's wisdom and plan for the nations is already at work in the earth. He is gathering as many who will receive His Son and His salvation into the ark of safety which is the new creation. If any man be in Christ, he is a new creation! Old things are passed away and behold all things are new! It is the heart of man that God is after. He changes it and thereby changes his very nature. It is the gift of God that He has given unto men! It is the gift of eternal life. This gift of eternal life is accompanied by many other gifts! Through God's gift of eternal life, He is able to birth in men ministry gifts that are so powerful; these gifts have been used to bring whole continents out of darkness into His eternal light. This life has changed nations socially, ideologically, educationally, economically, and politically, to the glory of God. This life has released God's manifold wisdom into the nations.

If you look at the nations that have embraced Jesus Christ, homes, villages, cities, and nations, you will see the nations that have been world leaders in economics, technology, civics, and education. I am talking about those nations that have regard for humanity and the right to exist as the free moral agents God created humanity to be. Through those nations, God has been able to reign His blessings upon the unjust nations as well. We see a surge in economics, culture, sociology, and technology, in countries that were very poor and under-developed, just several decades ago.

Through these changes and developments infrastructures have been developed to allow God an avenue into these nations to bring the light of His Truth and salvation that never would have been possible without the yielding of the hearts of men to His gift, and the gifts that made these monumental advancements possible! Make no mistake about it; all knowledge comes from God, and it is then disseminated by men to humanity for His good purpose.

God is out to bless because Jesus Christ has paid, in full, for the sins of the whole world! Through God's grace and wisdom, He is reaching the populations of the world, even the nations where it has been illegal to worship Christ; the Gospel has penetrated through satellite, the Internet, and social media, and more.

God gave gifts unto to men for the work of the ministry for the perfecting of His children and for the building up (edifying) of His people! We can attack one another on the lines of race, global interest, sexual orientation, just to name a few, but it is only Christ and His eternal unconditional love and His plan of redemption that will divinely resolve the flaws and faults of humanity. Humanity has not the wisdom, nor the resolve to combat the issues at hand. It will take the Creator to bring order and peace out of chaos in this hour.

As many as received Him (Jesus) gave He, power (authority) to become the sons of God. It is the new birth that recreates the human spirit to rescue fallen man from the perversion of darkness that is creating division and chaos, globally. It is the spirituality of the Lord God Almighty in the hearts of men who have been placed in the heart by the gift of God, Jesus Christ eternal life.

In 1 Corinthians 12, Paul is speaking, by the Spirit of God, addressing the lack of spiritual knowledge and understanding in the Church at Corinth concerning what we have in the body of Christ. If the Church at Corinth needed light concerning the spiritual heights of which we have ascended to in Christ, then the 21st Century Church needs to be taught concerning the spirituality of the body.

Paul, under the inspiration of the Holy Spirit, wrote concerning spiritual gifts. The word *gifts* is italicized in the *King James Version* of the Bible. See verse 1 of 1 Corinthians 12. This implies the word gifts was added to try and bring clarity to the writings. Paul spoke of nine gifts which are divided into three categories: they are revelation gifts, power gifts and vocal gifts. Now there are diversities of gifts, but the same Spirit. And there are differences of administrations, but the same Lord. And there are diversities of operations, but it is the same God which worketh all in all. However, the manifestation of the Spirit is given to every man to profit withal. The Scripture divides the gifts into three categories, and they are outlined as follows.

"And there are diversities of operations, but it is the same God which worketh all in all. But the manifestation of the Spirit is given to every man to profit withal. For to one is given by the Spirit the word of wisdom; to another the word of knowledge by the same Spirit; To another faith by the same Spirit; to another the gifts of healing by the same Spirit; To another the working of miracles; to another prophecy; to another discerning of spirits; to another divers kinds of tongues; to another the interpretation of tongues: But all these worketh that one and the selfsame Spirit, dividing to every man severally as he will." 1 Corinthians 12:6-11

The word spiritual was used in the original Greek, and it refers to God's supernatural wonder-working power that comes upon His people to work in the Kingdom to fulfill His will on the earth. It is the spiritual endowment of God given by the power of the Holy Spirit to empower the Church.

The power or the anointing gives us the divine ability to become workers together with God. The love of God has brought every member of His body into major significance with the Father. All are spiritually endowed, and all are needed and nurtured by the life of God. All can be used by the Holy Spirit to manifest or operate in these gifts. Because one is used by the Spirit to operate in the gifts does not mean that they are called to the five-fold ministry. The nine gifts can be manifested through any member of the body at any time. Notice the Scripture says in verse 11, "…the selfsame Spirit, dividing to every man severally as He will." So, it is not the will of man that these gifts manifest but the will of God by the Holy Spirit. All members of the body of Christ may not be fully mature Christians, but they can be used by the Holy Spirit to manifest the gifts of the Spirit for the work of the ministry of His body to the lost.

Though we all may not be seasoned or mature, we are all placed in the body by our Heavenly Father. We are tender and beloved in His sight. As we are taught the living Word by the Holy Spirit, we are transformed by the loving Word of God and we have become fit, for the Master's use, in the body.

The wonder and beauty of the transformation occurs as the Spirit supplies spiritual abundant life within the body of Christ. God has supplied gifts and administrations that will operate in the Church, supplying nutrients to every cell in His body. The Church continues to evolve into the fullness of Christ because it is God who is at work in us. We are strengthened by His might and receive a constant supply of the Spirit to minister the salvation of Christ to the world, reaping the fruit of the earth. Once the set level of maturity of the Church has been reached and the harvest is complete the Church will be presented as a chaste virgin unto the Father.

"And God hath set some in the church, first apostles, secondarily prophets, thirdly teachers, after that miracles, then gifts of healings, helps, governments, diversities of tongues." 1 Corinthians 12:28

Jesus taught the disciples for three and a half years. They handled the Word of life and fellowshipped with the Chief Apostle Jesus Christ. The apostles witnessed the authority of God in and upon Jesus as He cast out demonic spirits with His words. He spoke to the storms and the sea and they obeyed Him. Jesus walked on water, He raised the dead, He healed multitudes, and He fed the crowds miraculously and supernaturally.

His wisdom was irresistible as He went about exposing the shallow religious blind leaders of the day and His compassion was birthed out of a love that was lost to man in the garden. The cry went forth, that never a man spake like this man. Jesus did so many wonderful works and, if they were all written down, the Word declares that the world could not contain all the books that would be written.

People of religion and tradition will quickly declare that Jesus was able to do the mighty works because He was the Son of God. But the Word declares that Jesus stripped Himself of His mighty power and glory prior to coming into this world. He took upon Himself a human body. He became a man just as Adam was before the fall.

Jesus had the same physical immortality Adam had before he sinned and died spiritually. Jesus did no miracles until He became of legal age, which was 30 years old according to tradition. He submitted Himself to His parents until He reached adulthood. During those 30 years, prior to entering His ministry, He was sinless, spotless --the Holy Lamb of God. So, when John the Baptist saw Jesus approaching beyond the Jordan where he was baptizing, John cried, behold the Lamb of God who takes away the sin of the world! John was full of the Holy Ghost and the Spirit bore witness signifying that Jesus was the Holy Lamb ready to be baptized with power.

John felt unworthy to baptize the Holy Lamb of God. Jesus told John suffer it to be so to fulfill all righteousness, because the Scriptures must be fulfilled. So, when Jesus went into the Jordan and was submerged in baptism, He then arose, and the Holy Ghost descended like a dove upon Him. What a glorious moment in time it was when heaven's power came down and rested on the Son of Man, Jesus Christ. The Word declares He received the Spirit without measure. It was the anointing of the Holy Ghost that empowered Jesus to minister as a man filled with God. He demonstrated what we would be like once we were born of God and filled with the Holy Spirit. He wanted believers to understand that the works He did, we would do also, and greater works shall we do. See John 14:12

As soon as the Church was born the Holy Ghost came like a mighty rushing wind and sat upon the 120 in the upper room in the form of cloven tongues like as of fire! The gifts and administrations of the Spirit were immediately manifested in the lives of the men and women who were in the upper room. Peter, who was one of the apostles of the Lamb, began to operate in the apostolic anointing. He preached the Word right off the pages of Joel 2 and declared this is that which was spoken by the prophet Joel!

"And they were all amazed, and were in doubt, saying one to another, What meaneth this? Others mocking said, these men are full of new wine. But Peter, standing up with the eleven, lifted up his voice, and said unto them, Ye men of Judaea, and all ye that dwell at Jerusalem, be this known unto you, and hearken to my words: For these are not drunken, as ye suppose, seeing it is but the third hour of the day. But this is that which was spoken by the prophet Joel; And it shall come to pass in the last days, saith God, I will pour out of my Spirit upon all flesh: and your sons and your daughters shall prophesy, and your young men shall see visions, and your old men shall dream dreams: And on my servants and on my handmaidens I will pour out in those days of my Spirit; and they shall prophesy: And I will shew wonders in Heaven above, and signs in the earth beneath; blood, and fire, and vapour of smoke: The sun shall be turned into darkness, and the moon into blood, before that great and notable day of the Lord come: And it shall come to pass, that whosoever shall call on the name of the Lord shall be saved." (See Acts 2:12-22)

So immediately after the outpouring of the Holy Spirit we see the Church, which is the body of Christ being formed, and the spiritual gift of the apostleship operating in Peter; apostle simply means a sent one by God. About 3,000 souls were added to the Church on that day. The Scripture declares in Acts 2:42-43: "And they continued steadfastly in the apostles' doctrine and fellowship, and in breaking of bread, and in prayers. And fear came upon every soul: and many wonders and signs were done by the apostles."

An apostle of God who is called to operate in the true depths of that office will have signs and wonders following their ministry. There will always be an atmosphere of the miraculous when the office of the apostle is operating. So, it is obvious that the spiritual gift of apostleship was first, according to the Scripture and it came into manifestation in the life of Peter on the Day of Pentecost.

The office of the apostle is still operating in the body of Christ today. The original twelve apostles were called the apostles of the Lamb. These men were chosen by God to be taught personally by Christ and to witness the ministry of Christ, firsthand. So, the office or gift is still in effect but there will never be any more apostles of the Lamb. It should also be noted that with this ministry gift the apostle is usually accompanied by the power gifts of the Spirit, so it was the power of God that started the Church, and it is the power of God that will finish the full maturing of the Church, which is His body!

The apostle is used to pioneer new works and form local churches all over the world. Missionaries who have been sent and or called by God to the remote unchurched places in this world, operated in a measure of the gift or the anointing of the apostle. All apostles do not have the same measure of the ministry gift, as all pastors do not operate in the same measure of the anointing in their office. The measure of the gift and the anointing will be determined by the calling of God on the life of the individual and their level of consecration unto God. We must give ourselves completely to God and strive for the masteries. We press towards the prize of the high calling of God in Christ Jesus! Notice, the press is in Christ our Lord, the anointed one. It is a spiritually endowed supernatural press done in the strength of God --not the strength of men. This press is accomplished by consecrating our lives unto Him, no matter our career or purpose in life. We present our bodies a living sacrifice unto God so that He can maximize and glorify Christ in us. This commitment will cause us to reach the highest prize and reward possible for our commitment to His Kingdom.

As we accept whatever calling God has on our lives, we put our hands to the plow, and we should not look back. As we go forth the grace of God will suffice and empower us to minister with the ability that comes from the Father. As we go forth in obedience to God, we will find the resources of Heaven flowing freely into and through our lives.

As the rivers of life flow in and through us, we minister out of the supply of the Spirit. Jesus said out of your inner most being will flow rivers of living water. The water, referenced in the Scripture in John 7:38 is referring to the Holy Spirit flowing through the believer like a mighty river that will bring life and salvation to those who will receive it.

The Holy Spirit is the third person of the Trinity sent from Heaven to anoint us for whatever the call. Acts 10:38 says "How God anointed Jesus of Nazareth with the Holy Ghost and with power: who went about doing good and healing all that were oppressed of the devil; for God was with him." In Acts 1, Jesus told the disciples they were to be empowered by God. He said after the Holy Ghost has come upon you, you shall receive power to be witnesses in Jerusalem, Judea, Samaria and to the utter most parts of the earth. We see here these words spoken by Jesus were not just for the early Church, but for the latter Church as well. See Acts 1:8

Daniel said in the last days knowledge would increase upon the earth and those who do know their God shall be strong and do exploits. The words of Jesus spoken concerning the power of the Holy Ghost are still anointing and empowering believers all over the world. Men and women on every continent are responding to the call of the Lord and being filled with the Spirit.

The mature children of God are forsaking all the world has to offer, to host the presence and power of God. As we get closer to the end of the Church age, God's grace will lift us to new dimensions of His glory. We will walk in higher realms of His light. The Kingdom of God will cause many to operate at a heightened level of divine consciousness of the Spirit. The Gospel of Christ will continue to span the globe bringing power and sweeping the nations. The Church will continue to reign with Christ, creating divine ideology that will influence regions and nations that were long since dominated by the religions of this world. Armies cannot stop His Truth. Governments cannot deter His light. Cultures will not dilute or retard this mighty move of God in the earth. Jesus said the gates of hell will not prevail against this glorious triumphant Church. God said in these last days He would pour His Spirit out upon all flesh.

The Church is on the verge of a move of God that will totally eclipse all previously recorded revival history. The body of Christ will channel the fullness of the knowledge of the glory of the Lord into the nations. The marvelous light of God is shining forth as declared by Isaiah 60. "Arise, shine; for thy light is come, and the glory of the Lord is risen upon thee. For, behold, the darkness shall cover the earth, and gross darkness the people: but the Lord shall arise upon thee, and his glory shall be seen upon thee. And the Gentiles shall come to thy light, and kings to the brightness of thy rising." Isaiah 60:1-3

This glorious light and presence of God has been wonderfully manifested during certain moves of God through the centuries, but nothing will compare to what our Father has planned for the grand finale prior to the rapture of the Church.

Smith Wigglesworth was a preacher from England born in the late 19th Century. He is referred to as an apostle of faith. He said he would rather have the presence of God upon him for one minute than to have the whole world with a fence around it. When the true unadulterated power of God is in manifestation the beauty of God will be revealed and there is nothing on earth like it. His love is shocking and amazing when purely encountered. As stated by the Apostle Paul in the Scripture below, there is nothing that ranks with this kind of love once we have a true encounter. "For I am persuaded, that neither death, nor life, nor angels, nor principalities, nor powers, nor things present, nor things to come, Nor height, nor depth, nor any other creature, shall be able to separate us from the love of God, which is in Christ Jesus our Lord." Romans 8:38-39

Men, women and even children, when encountering the great love of the Father, will break away from the gravitational pull of the things of this earth. They will lose the fear of death because the perfect love of the

Father casts out fear. God comforts us with His divine love, and we explode with a courage on the inside that originates in Heaven. We have been freed from the corruption of the lusts of this world and we are given the grace of our Lord Jesus, to pursue the wonderful, glorious fellowship of His sufferings, and we may be found in Him and in His great love which sent Him to the cross.

John Wesley, the great founder of the Methodist movement, was entrenched in religion as a young man, and though He was an ordained minister he had never been born again. Wesley had not been born of God. It is possible for one to attend church all their life and never receive Christ as Savior and get born again. Jesus said to Nicodemus, you must be born again. There is a new birth and a baptism into Christ. I am speaking of God-ordained spiritual events that occur when we receive the Lordship of the Lamb. There are men and women who were zealously pursuing what they considered the will of God in ministry but had not been born of God, nor did they understand or know His calling for their lives.

Wesley was on board a ship bound for America when he encountered a group of believers called the Moravians. The Moravians walked in a level of divine humility and love that manifested the living Savior. While crossing the ocean a great storm arose. It appeared the ship was going to be destroyed and all the lives on board would be lost. As the ship was tossed by the winds and the waves the account says the Moravians began to sing and they showed no sign of fear or intimidation because of the great storm. Even the women and children remained calm and worshipped until the storm passed. Wesley knew after this observation that these children of God had something that was not of this world. They were filled with God's love, and when Wesley encountered that love he became thirsty for the living water. There is an encounter with God that changes the heart, forever. It is the work of the Holy Spirit that lights a fire in our hearts and brings us into intimate fellowship with the Lamb.

As for my own journey into this glorious Kingdom, it was also marred by tradition and religion, as opposed to a real encounter with the Savior. I cannot remember the first day I attended church as a child. It seems I went to church all my childhood. My mother was always insistent that we go, so we attended service every Sunday, it seemed. I recall my mother coming into the bedroom when I was around seven years of age one Sunday morning. She made me get up and get dressed for church, as usual. However, on this specific Sunday it seemed I was more irritated by her

58

insistence than usual. But to spare myself the pain of a spanking I thought it would be wise to consent without resistance. Growing up in Louisiana in the mid-sixties was a different era. The discipline exercised in the lives of children growing up in that era was more intrusive, to say the least. In my days as a child there was swift physical punishment for anything that resembled disobedience. There was no such thing as child abuse at that level. Even the neighbors were obliged to spank you or as we use to say beat you down if you were caught anywhere in the neighborhood misbehaving. Well, to finish my story, on this specific Sunday morning when I arrived at church, the Sunday school lesson was different somehow; something divine or heavenly happened to me as I was listening to the teacher. I felt as if I was literally walking on air as I left church that morning. The anointing of God came on me, and as a young seven year-old boy, I was so over joyed by the experience and I still remember it so vividly today, over fifty years later – just like it was yesterday. I recall thinking to myself that I must have been crazy not to have wanted to go to church because of that experience. Please note that this specific denominational church I attended at the time did not believe in any type of manifestations of the Holy Spirit. They did not even allow instruments in the church. We would sing songs out of the hymnals without a piano or organ. To date, they still have the same order. Nevertheless, the Spirit of God met me in this setting and revealed His presence and beauty in a manner that I will never forget. God's love is always searching the earth for those who will receive His grace. He wants to show forth His love and strength. We see this desire of our Lord, reflected in the Scripture below:

"For the eyes of the Lord run to and fro throughout the whole earth, to show himself strong in the behalf of them whose heart is perfect toward him." 2 Chronicles 16:9

At the age of 16, I had another encounter with God's presence. I was launched into an even greater reality of God's love and power. I met a half-sister of mine who had been living in California. We have the same father but different mothers. We were first introduced to one another as teenagers. My sister had been filled with the Spirit of God in her early teens and was very committed to studying God's Word. When we all sat around in my father's home watching television my sister would sit quietly studying the Bible. I was captivated and amazed that anyone her age could ignore the distractions of this world and commune with God by constantly reading His Word. This greatly impacted my life and created a hunger in me to also know the same level of fellowship with God.

I did not understand the spiritual ramifications of such a lifestyle. I did not know it was the grace and love of God that created such relationships. I did not know that it is the work of the Holy Spirit that leads us into that place of love for the Father and His Word. The more I questioned her about her faith the more I thirst for this living water. Well, after a long visit with us over the summer she returned to California. But the seed had already been planted. I was hungry for what she had. There was a King James Version of the Bible in my home, so I started in the Book of Genesis. My plan was to read and devour the Bible from Genesis to Revelation. Well, after reading several paragraphs into the first chapter of the Book of Genesis I became a little discouraged because I was trying to use my intellect to get acquainted with God through His Word. This of course is impossible because these are matters of the Spirit.

In the Gospel of John 4, Jesus had a conversation at the well with the woman of Samaria. He asked the woman for a drink of water from the well. She was surprised that Jesus, who was a Jew, would have a conversation with a Samaritan, because Samaritans were out casts. But Jesus continued the conversation by telling the woman if she had asked Him for water, He would have given her water that would cause her never to thirst again. The woman was thinking naturally but Jesus was speaking spiritually. She said to Jesus, give me this water so that I will never thirst again. The encounter is noted below:

"He told her, "Go, call your husband and come back." "I have no husband," she replied. Jesus said to her, "You are right when you say you have no husband. The fact is, you have had five husbands, and the man you now have is not your husband. What you have just said is quite true. "Sir," the woman said, "I can see that you are a prophet. Our ancestors worshiped on this mountain, but you Jews claim that the place where we must worship is in Jerusalem." "Woman," Jesus replied, "believe me, a time is coming when you will worship the Father neither on this mountain nor in Jerusalem. You Samaritans worship what you do not know; we worship what we do know, for salvation is from the Jews. Yet a time is coming and has now come when the true worshipers will worship the Father in the Spirit and in Truth, for they are the kind of worshipers the Father seeks. God is spirit, and his worshipers must worship in the Spirit and in truth." John 4:16-24 *New International Version*

Jesus used a natural reference to bring forth a very powerful spiritual truth. Physically our bodies need water to survive. Water sustains life and helps replenish the body naturally. Jesus enlightened her then, and He continues to enlighten the Church today through His conversation with the Samaritan woman at the well in His Word. He wants us to know we can drink from the living waters of the well of salvation. This living water satisfies a thirst that is in the heart of man. It brings a spiritual renewal and a door into the Kingdom of God. This living water will bring us to a spiritual awakening and a place of worship unto the true living God in our spirits. We gain a consciousness of the inner man, which is the real man.

Our spiritual senses come alive in us, allowing us to fellowship with Christ. We worship Him in spirit and in truth. We drink and we are filled with divine life in our spirits. The psalmist said taste and see that the Lord is good. We taste of the abundant life of Christ with our spirit. We allow the spirit to gain the ascendency over the intellect. We start living by faith because faith is of the Spirit. The just shall live by faith. Without a drink of the living water, it is impossible to know this highest reality. You can mentally ascend to facts and information concerning Jesus or the Kingdom, but it will not yield eternal life. Mental ascension will not bring forth the new birth; it is when we have an encounter with God a Spirit, with our spirits. It is the revelation of information that is downloaded into our hearts that bring us into fellowship and dominion in Christ Jesus. We are translated out of darkness into the Kingdom of His Dear Son when we drink of the waters of Heaven, freely.

So as a 16-year-old young boy, I finally had an encounter with God through my spirit in a greater measure. I could not get enough of the Gospels. I read the Bible both day and night. My mother was concerned that I took such a deep interest in the Word of God. She came into my bedroom one night while I was reading and voiced her concern. She told me that while she was pleased that I had taken an interest in reading the Bible, she was concerned that I was reading it too much; she told me I needed to get out and do the fun things other kids my age were doing. I smiled, but as soon as she left the room I went right back to my reading because I was continuously overjoyed in spending quality time with God. At that time I was reading John 14, and when I came to verse 12, it was as if the verse leaped off the page into my heart. Jesus made this declaration:

"I assure you, most solemnly I tell you, if anyone steadfastly believes in Me, he will himself be able to do the things that I do; and he will do even greater things than these, because I go to the Father." John 14:12, *Amplified Bible Classic Edition*

The reality of what Jesus said in this Scripture exploded into pure life in my spirit. I was conscious of a reality that was more real than what I knew mentally or physically. I stood up and declared out loud, *"Lord, they have not been teaching this in my church!"* I stood in the middle of my bedroom that night and I asked the Lord to let me know His Spirit. I knew there was something far deeper to know of and about God than what I had previously experienced. Suddenly, a divine presence began to fill the ceiling of my room. This is the very moment I became aware of my inner spirit, the inner man. There was a consciousness of my inner-most being occurring at the very same time His divine presence filled the ceiling of my room. It was not my physical senses that made me aware of the presence of God --it was my inner man or my spirit man which seemed to come alive with heightened sensitivity to the Spirit of God.

Then there was a gentle touch at the top of my head, and it seemed like perfection began to flow through every part of my spirit, soul, and body. For the first time in my existence, I felt complete and perfect. There was no inferiority or fear in any part of my being. I now know today that it was the abundant life of Christ that flowed into me, and it is absolutely impossible to exaggerate the love I experienced during this encounter with Him.

In John 14:12, Jesus told His followers they could walk at a level of grace that would take them into a realm of ministry and works He, Jesus, had already known on the earth, and even greater works. This is a divine truth straight from the Throne of God that has been released into the Church to nourish us in our spirits until there is an explosion of light that will propel us into the greater works, and beyond. Isaiah 55 states the following:

"So shall my word be that goeth forth out of my mouth: it shall not return unto me void, but it shall accomplish that which I please, and it shall prosper in the thing whereto I sent it." Isaiah 55:11

Jesus said, "For I have not spoken of myself; but the Father which sent me, he gave me a commandment, what I should say, and what I should speak." John 12:49

So, we see the Word of the Lord from the Prophet Isaiah and from our Lord and Savior declaring the creative reality that comes into our hearts when we receive the Word of the Lord. The Word produces and creates what is spoken from the Throne of God. Because we believe the Word of God we have come into infinite light, power, and authority. We are moving toward that place of seeing all things placed under His feet which is His body. This is the ordained activity of the body of Christ in the earth by our Father in Heaven.

The Lord takes pleasure in illuminating our hearts with light. The spirit of man is the candle of the Lord searching all the inward parts of the belly. We are called into oneness with the Father so that He may fill us with so much life until Jesus is constantly glorified in our mortal bodies.

There is no substitute in the believer's heart for the Spirit of God. What power and blessing we forfeit when we grieve the Spirit of the Lord by allowing the influence of the flesh and the world to distance us from His care and comfort. God is calling us into the deeper places of His presence.

We are not orphans, and we are not left to try and make it on our own, but we have been given the earnest of the Spirit. We have been sealed by His grace through faith to fellowship with the Holy Trinity until so much of Jesus is shining forth in us. The very atmosphere will be charged with Heaven's glory. All of hell trembles at the thought of mature sons of God walking on the earth. We become wise master builders, working together as one with our Heavenly Father. We walk as vessels of honor filled with divine humility, yet possessing great authority and the pureness of His love.

Before the return of Christ there will be men, woman, boys, and girls who are so filled with Heaven's blessings that constant manifestations of God's power will be seen at levels that will satisfy the thirst of hungry hearts all over this planet.

There are dominions of both the Kingdom realm and the Spiritual realm that have not been touched by the Spirit-filled church yet. God has preserved such places and moves of His Spirit for these last days. The river of life is flowing faster and deeper than ever. The Father is inviting us to abandon ourselves and flow freely in the river, and to allow the river to flow freely through us, and where the river of the Lord flows, it will bring a manifestation of the pure life of our Heavenly Father.

The fire of God will fall on us like rain, burning and removing the impurities of the world from our lives. Father God, who is jealous for us, will rush into us like a mighty flood as we allow the fire of God to make room for Him in our hearts and in our minds. All of God's love, power, provisions, grace, mercy, riches, and glory are toward us as the Scripture declares: "By having the eyes of your heart flooded with light, so that you can know and understand the hope to which He has called you, and how rich is His glorious inheritance in the saints (His set-apart ones), And [so that you can know and understand] what is the immeasurable and unlimited and surpassing greatness of His power in and for us who believe, as demonstrated in the working of His mighty strength,". This Scripture declares our blessed place of inheritance. Ephesians 1:18-19, *Amplified Bible Classic Edition*

"And He raised us up together with Him and made us sit down together [giving us joint seating with Him] in the heavenly sphere [by virtue of our being] in Christ Jesus (the Messiah, the Anointed One). He did this that He might clearly demonstrate through the ages to come the immeasurable (limitless, surpassing) riches of His free grace (His unmerited favor) in [His] kindness and goodness of heart toward us in Christ Jesus."
Ephesians 2:6-7, *Amplified Bible Classic Edition*

So, we see our spirits have already been raised up together with Him in the heavenly Holy of Holies. And in the ages and eternity to come, God our Father will continually flood us with light, truth, riches, and pleasures untold.

There is nothing in the natural that can compare to what awaits us on earth or in the Heaven of heavens as we give our all to Him. Peter calls it joy unspeakable and full of glory. It is the prepared place for the redeemed of the Lord.

There is an excitement brewing in the Kingdom of God. We have seen, and we are still seeing the worst of times coming upon the earth; we see the wars and rumors of wars spoken of by Jesus to His disciples when He prophetically spoke of end time events. We see plagues, viruses (COVID 19, Ebola) and other diseases. The events in the Middle East continue to move the world toward the eventual concerted effort to try and eliminate Israel. God will turn back the enemies of Zion supernaturally and the world will know that JEHOVAH reigns, and He is the God of Israel. For the world system shall continue in corruption before our very eyes.

But make no mistake! The best of times is manifesting here on the earth among the people of God. Those who are born of the seed of the incorruptible Word of God will be immersed into Christ, receiving the engrafted Word which anchors, restores, preserves, and saves the soul.

The Church is growing in the reality of the love of God. There is a pureness of life laying hold of the Church that cannot be denied because the supernatural working of God's power is growing stronger to usher in a people on the earth who will walk as Jesus walked. We shall walk in the same Spirit as when He walked on the earth as a man filled with God. We are being transformed into His very image from one dimension of glory to another. We are liberated continually into the brightness of His very being. We the people of God –the Church --are growing in intimacy of Spirit with the Lord of Host.

Though tribulation will come to the Church, it will always result in jubilation for those who have been graced by God to stand firm --having done all to stand. We are walking in the strength of God and cannot be deterred by the temporary circumstances of this life. We are soldiers in the Army of the Living God. We are a mighty moving deliberate force from above that will dominate in the earth until every enemy of light has been placed under the feet of Christ and the Church. We are workers together with Christ, the head of the Church to destroy all the works of the devil.

Prayer

Father, we submit to your plans and purpose for this hour concerning the Church. We submit to your Lordship Jesus and to the gifts you gave unto to men when you ascended on high. Father thank you for raising up seasoned enlightened ministry gifts that are leading the Church to new dimensions of prayer, grace and glory. Thank you for the elect and those having the end of their faith, Jesus Christ, the same yesterday, today and forever.

Highlights

1. Jesus is the Chief Shepard and head of this glorious triumphant Church.

2. It is through the special equipping and provisions to the Church by the supply of the Spirit that gives the Church the power to do ministry in the earth. The Scripture declares it's not by might nor by power but it's by my Spirit says the Lord. Zechariah 4:6

3. If the Church is to reach full maturity it will be through the ministry of those men and women who have not just received gifts from on high, but to those who give themselves whole heartedly to the call, through constant prayer, consecration, and study of the Word. Also, receiving the seasoned leaders who God has placed in the Church, past and present, to help mature those called into ministry.

Reflection & Discussion Questions

1. How does the Gospel impact the soul of continents and nations?

2. What is God's plan for this fallen creation?

3. Has God given up on humanity and did God bring the current world problems into existence?

4. What is God's plan for fallen humanity?

Chapter 5

Filled with His Spirit

The greatest privilege known to humanity is to be born of God and to be filled with His Spirit. Jesus told His disciples that He was going away prior to His death, burial, and resurrection. Jesus stated it was expedient that He go away.

It was to the advantage of the disciples, and to the whole world, that Jesus Christ ascend to Heaven, into the very Throne Room of God and atone for the sins of the earth by sprinkling His blood on the altar of Jehovah God. The atonement through Christ opened a portal in the heavens, allowing humanity and all of creation to be reunited with the Creator and Father of Spirits. The Scripture says seals were broken on the book that was in the hand of God by the Lamb that had been slain. No one in Heaven, in the earth nor under the earth was found worthy to open this great book of mysteries, and the power that was to reclaim creation and destroy the works of darkness, thereby bringing forth judgment; even the end of the rule of Satan on the earth. The judgment will be on all those, both angels and man, who have rejected the Lamb and rejected His salvation. Satan and the fallen angels rejected the glorious Creator and the awesome love that created them. Everything was created by His Word and without the Word, was nothing made.

Man, after his fall through Adam and because of his earthly habitation, was given a chance through the loving Savior, Jesus, to be redeemed, but not to his original earthly domain, but to a heavenly domain.

Satan fell from the very Throne Room of God where he was privileged to walk in the very fire under God's Throne. Iniquity was found in Satan. His pride brought rebellion and he took one third of God's angels with him. Thus, he no longer has access to the glorious fire of God, and he is destined for the fires of hell. But God has something far better for those who have received Jesus, the King of glory. He has sent the Holy Spirit to the earth to make us new creations and to fill us with power! The Spirit of God (Holy Spirit) was sent to the earth as like a rushing mighty wind and fire on the Day of Pentecost in that upper room where 120 disciples of Jesus Christ had been told by Him to go to the upper room in Jerusalem and wait; they were to wait for the Holy Ghost and power. It was the

Spirit of God that ascended into the earth on that awe-inspiring blessed day, bringing the power that was to fuel the Kingdom of His Son, that was to explode and expand in the earth, drawing every tongue, kindred, and nation into this new creation.

It is the Kingdom of God's Dear Son, who is the first born of many children. The preparation of the Church has been accelerated to prepare the people of God to operate in Sonship to God our Father. So that the Church may reach her full zenith on the earth, those who have been placed into the body of Christ must go into the inner courts of the spiritual sanctuary, but we must not stop there at the inner court. We must go on with God into the Holy of Holies. In the Old Testament we have the types and shadows of the Church demonstrated in the temple that was built by Solomon. The temple consisted of the outer court, the inner court, and the Holy of Holies. The three-part temple references can be correlated to the three stages of spiritual encounters that the individual believer can transition through.

Obviously the first and most important transition we need is to be born of God by the incorruptible seed of the Word. In this transition we are placed in the body of Christ, and we receive divine adoption into the family of our Heavenly Father. This is something far beyond what happens on a natural order when a natural family adopts a child. The child adopted into the natural family can receive all the legal rights and status of a family member. The child can receive the same nourishing and care as the biological child in the family. But there can never and will never be a transition where the child takes on the DNA of the adoptive parents. The adopted child can never have the blood of the parents. Now of course we do not make light of the commitment and love that can develop in such relationships, and if the adopting parents are believers, then there is a more divine, eternal love that is working in the midst of that family to form a nucleus in which God is the center.

But I want to emphasize what happens when God adopts and engrafts us into His household of faith. First, we must understand that Adam was called the son of God and he was of the same stock, spiritually, as God, before the fall. Without going into much detail here, let's consider the natural family and natural parents. When a child is born into a family the child receives the same physical, psychological, biological traits of the parents. The child will grow up displaying the same behavior patterns of the parents, and of course, the child will also bare the resemblance of the

68

parents. So consequently, the child is equipped with everything needed to fellowship and commune with the parents on a level that is uninhibited because they are of the same stock.

Now consider God, who we know is the Creator of all creation, and when it came to man, God was looking to start a family. He spoke the universe and everything in it into existence, but with man He released out of Himself the breath of life (zoe). Man became a living soul. Man was of the same stock as God, and he was brought forth to create.

The reason we have the many disciplines and professions of life on this planet is because we are created in His image. All so called civilization, arts, cities, cultures, family structure, laws and anything that contributes to the social wellbeing of humanity exist because we are of the stock of God. When man was restored to God after the resurrection of Christ, sin no longer separated us from the Father. Only our denial of the blood of the Lamb keeps us a prisoner to the fallen nature. Without the new birth through the Word of God Satan is the father of fallen man's spirit and he is in the kingdom of darkness. In this new life of God, we are speaking spirits! We are like our spiritual Father as much as Jesus is like Him in our spirits. We are His offspring and when we accepted the finished work of Christ, we gave God the Father the right to reclaim us and recreate our human spirits. God, through the finished work of Christ, has put us right back into the same class, spiritually, as He is! Jesus Christ has become our righteousness. Through the gift of righteousness in Christ Jesus we have right standing with God. We have come into divine fellowship and sweet communion with our Heavenly Father by the precious blood of Jesus. We have been born of God by the incorruptible seed of the Word. We are the manifested Sons of God. No, we are not God, we are like God! Our spirit or inner man has become a new creation as we referenced earlier. The Scripture declares the following:

"Behold, what manner of love the Father hath bestowed upon us, that we should be called the sons of God: therefore the world knoweth us not, because it knew him not. Beloved, now are we the sons of God, and it doth not yet appear what we shall be: but we know that, when he shall appear, we shall be like him; for we shall see him as he is."
1 John 3:1-2

So, we are as much the Son of God as Jesus is the Son of God, by the Father's own design. It is God reconciling us as His children. We have received His Spirit of adoption whereby we cry Abba, Father. See Romans 8:15. We have been translated out of the kingdom of darkness into the Kingdom of His Dear Son, Jesus.

God the Father is calling us to grow up into all things in Jesus Christ so that we can operate in the same manner as our elder brother Jesus did in His three and a half years of ministry here on the earth. We have our Heavenly Father's spiritual DNA, and not many days hence, we will have the Father's DNA in our new spiritual bodies. For we shall be changed in a moment, in the twinkling of an eye, we shall be like Jesus. See 1 Corinthians 15:51–52.

The second spiritual transition consists of going into the inner court. The inner court is receiving the baptism of the Holy Spirit. When a person is born again (born of God) the Holy Spirit comes into his/her spirit to live. So, when we are born again the Spirit of God comes to reside forever in us. The Holy Spirit came to live on the inside of us, and to lead and guide us into all Truth. He came to teach, comfort, strengthen, counsel, and help us! It is the Holy Spirit in our recreated born-again spirit that helps us to live a successful life both spiritually and naturally, as we submit and yield to Him. The Holy Spirit within reminds us of the Word of God and brings all things to our remembrance. See John 14:26.

But when we are baptized in the Holy Spirit the Spirit of God comes upon us and we are filled with the Holy Spirit. To be filled with the Holy Spirit is to be filled with God. To be filled with the Holy Spirit is to be filled with the power of God. He equips us with His mighty power. As we operate in cooperation with the Holy Spirit we work as co-laborers with our Heavenly Father. Jesus told His disciples prior to His ascension into Heaven to go and wait in the upper room in Jerusalem until they were endued with power from on high. Jesus told them that after the Holy Ghost has come upon you, you shall receive power to be witnesses in Jerusalem, Judea, Samaria and to the uttermost parts of the earth. It is the infilling of God's power by the Holy Spirit that gives us the divine ability needed to fulfill the great commission Jesus gave when He said go ye into all the earth and teach the Good News of the Gospel to all nations – to everyone! See Matthew 28:18-20.

By the new birth and the infilling of the Holy Spirit we are brought into a reality of oneness with the Holy Trinity that lifts us far above the weak and beggarly elements of this world. We are lifted into His glory where the transfiguration is constant so that we are changed daily, from glory to glory. Our dependency is not of this world, nor our own limitations and means. We are equipped and empowered by the Holy Spirit. The weapons of our warfare are not carnal. We have been given the whole armor of God. These weapons and armor are not natural, nor are they earthly. We are clothed with a heavenly light. By the Holy Spirit we put on the Belt of Truth, we put on the Breastplate of Righteousness (we have received the gift of Righteousness), we shod our Feet with the Gospel of Peace, we take up the Shield of Faith and we crush every fiery dart (test, trials, and circumstances) of the enemy. We put on the Helmet of Salvation (knowing that we are redeemed) from the curse of this fallen creation and redeemed unto the blessing of Abraham and the Seed who is Christ! We take up the Sword of the Spirit which is God's Holy Word spoken out of our mouths by the inspiration of the Holy Ghost, who brings all Truth to our remembrance.

What glorious armor of light we have been given by the Holy Spirit who was sent to help us complete our pilgrimage as believers on the earth. We are Sons of God --even the redeemed of the Lord! By this infilling of the Holy Spirit, we have entered the realm of God our Father where nothing is impossible. When we are clothed with the power of Heaven by the Spirit's infilling, we become a god unto Satan and his kingdom because we are operating in the supremacy of the victorious Lamb.

The Scripture declares for this cause was the Son of God manifested that He might destroy the works of the devil. See 1 John 3:8. The Church is Christ's, and we are bone of His bone and flesh of His flesh, so we are on the earth to destroy the works of the devil, and the gates of hell cannot prevail against the Church.

The kingdom of Satan has no defense against the Church of the living God! We are more than conquerors. The Word of God declares the following, of Christ:

"And I beheld, and I heard the voice of many angels round about the throne and the beasts and the elders: and the number of them was ten thousand times ten thousand, and thousands of thousands; Saying with a loud voice, worthy is the Lamb that was slain to receive power, and riches, and wisdom, and strength, and honor, and glory, and blessing."
Revelation 5:11-12

Jesus was given power, riches, wisdom, strength, honor, glory, and blessing. Whatever Jesus has received we have received also because we are joint heirs together with Him!

"The Spirit itself beareth witness with our spirit, that we are the children of God: And if children, then heirs; heirs of God, and joint-heirs with Christ; if so be that we suffer with him, that we may be also glorified together." Romans 8:16-17

We also see that Jesus, fresh from His resurrection, declared in His Word, that all power is given unto Him in Heaven and in earth, and that we are to go into all the world and preach the Gospel. Jesus has delegated the Church authority in the following passages of Scripture.

"And he said unto them, Go ye into all the world, and preach the gospel to every creature. He that believeth and is baptized shall be saved; but he that believeth not shall be damned. And these signs shall follow them that believe; In my name shall they cast out devils; they shall speak with new tongues; They shall take up serpents; and if they drink any deadly thing, it shall not hurt them; they shall lay hands on the sick, and they shall recover. So then after the Lord had spoken unto them, he was received up into heaven, and sat on the right hand of God. And they went forth, and preached everywhere, the Lord working with them, and confirming the word with signs following. Amen." Mark 16:15-20

The third spiritual transitioning occurs when we go into the Holy of Holies. Going into the Holy of Holies simply means being filled with the Spirit and going on into the depths of fellowship and communion with God. In the Old Testament the high priest entered the Holy of Holies once a year to sacrifice on behalf of himself and for Israel's sins. The high priest entered in with the blood of animals to cover the sins of Israel so that God could bless and protect them, because the sin that separated them from God was covered by the blood of the sacrifice, according to the Old Testament. Note: God required animal sacrifices as a way for His people to temporarily atone for their sin. However, in the New Testament or the New Covenant, Jesus is the High Priest and the sacrifice. When Jesus was raised from hell, after He satisfied the claims of God's justice through His death on the cross --through His descension into hell -- through His ascension into the Throne Room of God which is the true Heavenly Holy of Holies, Jesus sprinkled His own blood on God's mercy seat for the remission of sin for the people; not to just cover sin but He forever wiped out sin, bridging humanity back to the Father of Spirits! (See Hebrews 9:22-28.) He blazed a trail into the Holy of Holies forever for us! If you confess with your mouth the Lord Jesus and believe in your heart that God has raised Him from the dead, you receive salvation which includes Sonship. We can now come boldly to God's Throne of Grace, to receive grace to help in times of need! (See Hebrews 4:16.) We, the saints of the Most-High God, have been redeemed forever and reconciled unto the Creator of the heavens and the earth! We are His dear children and His beloved!

There is absolutely no greater place to live than living in the presence of Almighty God, being comforted by His loving Spirit. It is the blood of Christ and the Holy Spirit that makes this lifestyle of entering the Holy of Holies possible. Many believers have found themselves raptured into God's Holy presence. But few have continued in the grace that allows them to abide in a lifestyle of constant Holy communion with the precious Lamb and the Father through the Holy Spirit.

The initial infilling of the Spirit ushers every believer into a reality that opens the door to the supernatural manifestations of the Spirit. It is the secret place of the Most-High God. The experience takes us into His beauty and presence. For days all we want is God, and we feel as though the whole world will have to know this greatness –that they would want to know this greatness, of what we have experienced. There are so many voices in the world that compete for the attention of the believer, to distract and desensitize the believer from the voice of the Holy Spirit speaking to our hearts. God gave us a perfect new heart when we were born again and placed His Spirit in us so that we could have power and strength to resist every enemy of faith that would try to keep us from the Holy of Holies.

When the Agape love (unconditional love) of God is given, the freedom of expression in our lives is a divine love affair with the Holy Trinity, and when this love is divinely manifested, there is nothing in any realm to compare with it. To sit at His feet and receive the wisdom that flows from God, which is first and foremost peaceable, gentle, and easy to be entreated, and full of good works and without partiality. There is a Holy reverence always growing in the heart of the child of God who chooses to dwell in the Holy place. An intimacy beyond anything natural is nurtured in the realm of the Spirit. The heart is lost in divine love and constantly crying out in an ecstasy of glory. In this state of glory, we are impregnated with knowledge, revelation, light, truth, and ministry. Everything in us is transformed, and Jesus Himself is glorified in our mortal bodies.

Prayer is continual, though much of it is unconscious because we are in Holy divine fellowship with the Father of Spirits. Praise will flow freely out of our hearts unto the Throne of our Lord. Everything in our lives becomes Throne centered because we live in a reality that is far above this earthly finite three-dimensional realm. God our Father is calling us to deeper places in His Kingdom, this moment, as you read this Book. He is calling you to a deeper level of grace. It is a cry that goes deep into the heart of the believer. It cannot be answered by the intellect. It goes way beyond the emotions and defies any circumstances that would try to impede His love toward us. If we open up to His love, it will sweep us into a place of abundant life where hidden treasures untold are endlessly our possession.

The Song of Solomon 2:10 says "My beloved spake, and said unto me, Rise up, my love, my fair one, and come away." God is calling us into a deep, rich intimacy and intercourse with Him so that we are constantly reproducing after Him in the earth. He wants us to be fruitful branches and trees of righteousness. We are to unleash the forces of Heaven upon the earth until all enemies have been placed under the feet of Christ.

There are moves of God waiting to explode in the earth that will be birthed out of the intimacy that occurs in the life of those who live in the Holy of Holies. No, everyone will not accept the call to deep intimacy in Him at this level, but those who will accept shall be called world changers and will transform nations. They shall do great exploits, and many will be birthed into the Kingdom of God because of the travailing prayers and works of those who dwell in the Holy of Holies, for they are the New Testament priests of the Most-High God. Isaiah declares the following:

"Who hath heard such a thing? Who hath seen such things? Shall the earth be made to bring forth in one day? Or shall a nation be born at once? For as soon as Zion travailed, she brought forth her children." Isaiah 66:8

Zion, again, is the Church in the New Testament. Isaiah is speaking prophetically about the Church living intimately with the Father in a place so Holy that our hearts would be filled with the compassion of the Lord.

The Father's intimacy with us will cause us to travail in prayer and birth in many into His Kingdom. Many will be translated into the Kingdom of His Dear Son because of the spiritual sacrifices offered up through the travailing hearts of those who live in the Holy of Holies.

What a wonderful privilege we have been afforded through Christ. We can live in the reality of our Father God, entering daily into the Holy place to live and serve as sons and daughters here upon the earth. We are one Spirit with the Lord, and yet, we are so disconnected at times from the true life of God, because of desensitization. The Church has not been taught the value of relationship and intimacy. We have not learned the true depth of His true love and revelation.

The time is short. God is quickening the Church with lightning speed to prepare an army of faithful believers who will rise-up strong in grace. We will walk continuously in the power of this new life. This end time of the outpouring of the Spirit, power and knowledge of the Lord will cause the Church to be transfigured right before the eyes of all her enemies, and great fear shall come upon the earth because of the army of the living God.

God's wisdom will be revealed and demonstrated through the Church. I am referring to the wisdom that brings the wisdom of this world to nothing. It is our spiritual life in Christ that makes us partakers of divine wisdom. Jesus's death on the cross was the wisdom of God to restore the bridge between Heaven and humanity. Through the wisdom of the cross, which seems foolish to fallen creation, humanity has been given a way of escape from sin, as noted in the Scripture below.

"For the message of the cross is foolishness to those who are perishing, but to us who are being saved it is the power of God. For it is written: I will destroy the wisdom of the wise; the intelligence of the intelligent I will frustrate. Where is the wise person? Where is the teacher of the law? Where is the philosopher of this age? Has not God made foolish the wisdom of the world? For since in the wisdom of God the world through its wisdom did not know him, God was pleased through the foolishness of what was preached to save those who believe." 1 Corinthians 1:18-21 *New International Version*

Also, see verses 28-29. "God chose the lowly things of this world and the despised things—and the things that are not—to nullify the things that are, so that no one may boast before him." The citizens of the Kingdom will dominate in every arena of life. There will be no field or profession where the wisdom of God will not flow through His children, causing them to rule and reign in life in Christ Jesus. Humanity has been offered deliverance unto perfection by the blood of Jesus. Those who have crossed the blood line by receiving the salvation of the Lamb are complete in Christ. There is no limit to what we can accomplish in Christ because His power is infinite. Again, I want to reiterate that we are beyond where Adam was before the fall. The Word also states that there was no greater than John the Baptist, but the least in the Kingdom is greater than John. The Scriptures declare that we are the manifested Sons of God. We will portray the God characteristics in this last hour.

Now we can understand why there has been such a fight to keep the Church in a babyhood state through divisions, strife, and discord. When we lose sight of the head of the Church, Jesus Christ, we lose our identity and we take on the false identity of lost humanity that is full of the destructive nature of their father, Satan. But the reality of the truth is that we have been born from above, right out of the loins of God by the incorruptible seed of the Word. We are moving deeper into the Holy of Holies where we fellowship and commune with the Most-High God, and we are continually moving from one glorious dimension to another. We will be changed in a moment, and in the twinkling of an eye. We have already put on immortality in our spirits but now we will put on immortality in our bodies. We are and shall be like God.

When God called Moses to go back into Egypt to deliver the children of Israel, He placed on him an anointing for the spectacular supernatural. As God spoke to Moses on the mount prior to Moses' return to Egypt, God's words created a god status on Moses; a miraculous power and authority was released upon him. The supernatural spectacular became a common occurrence in his life. We see in Exodus where God declared the following: "And the Lord said unto Moses, See, I have made thee a god to Pharaoh: and Aaron thy brother shall be thy prophet. Thou shalt speak all that I command thee: and Aaron thy brother shall speak unto Pharaoh, that he send the children of Israel out of his land." Exodus 7:1-2

We notice also that Jesus quoted Psalm 82:6 when He declared unto the Jews the following Truth stated in John 10. "Jesus answered them, Is it not written in your law, I said, Ye are gods? If he called them gods, unto whom the word of God came, and the Scripture cannot be broken;". John 10:34-35

God is sovereign, eternal and from everlasting to everlasting, He is the Almighty God. We are created in His image. Through the finished work of Christ, a door was opened to welcome home the prodigal son, which is fallen humanity! He has placed a ring, not on our finger, but in and around our hearts. The ring is Agape love, and He has robed us with His glory. We have in and on our inner man the anointing of God --even the Holy Spirit. We are sealed by God our Father and declared restored to a place of divine family honor. We are marked for greatness, and it is time to wake up and fulfill our destiny as His children in the earth.

Let the earth rejoice and the people be glad because Jesus has paved the way home, even into the very Throne Room of our Father. There is jubilation in Heaven and on earth among the redeemed of the Lord. There is a celebration and excitement among the angels of God as they witness the awesome grace that has come to earth. The people of God are walking more like Him and talking more like Him, more than ever. We are imitators of God.

"We having the same spirit of faith, according as it is written, I believed, and therefore have I spoken; we also believe, and therefore speak;" 2 Corinthians 4:13

We are taking authority over the works of darkness. We are causing the principalities and powers of darkness to scatter in terror because the Day of the Lord is at hand. This is the day the Lord has made! This manifestation of His power through His children is the sign of His imminent return to reclaim all of creation. So let us praise our KING! Let us call upon the NAME of our GOD! He will answer by fire! It is the fire of the Holy Ghost and power! The all-consuming fire of God is here on the earth, and we will see the increase thereof until all the wood, hay and stubble of our lives have been totally consumed.

"Wherefore we receiving a kingdom which cannot be moved, let us have grace, whereby we may serve God acceptably with reverence and godly fear: For our God is a consuming fire." Hebrews 12:28-29

Prayer

Father we thank you for the new birth, the in filling of your Spirit and the privilege to enter into the Holy of Holies. Fill us daily with your Spirit so that your Spirit of wisdom and revelation will give us greater intimacy with you and that we may know you even the more in a greater measure --the power that raised Jesus from the dead. Continue to flood the eyes of our understanding with light! Bring us into full transfiguration and transformation. Bring us into the fullness of the measure of the stature of Christ!

Highlights

1. The new birth lifts us into the New Creation in Christ Jesus, making us God's family.

2. Being filled with the Holy Spirit brings us into the power and manifestations of God's Spirit. Through this experience we are empowered to do the works Jesus did, and even greater works.

3. Living in God's presence we have access to the deeper realms of God, called the Holy of Holies. This is a place of deep rich fellowship with the Trinity and intimacy that brings great fruitfulness in and to His children on earth!

Reflection & Discussion Questions

1. Why does humanity need the new birth?

2. What is the new birth and how is it received?

3. What is the difference between the new birth and being filled with the Spirit?

Chapter 6

Grace for Grace

Another divine ingredient that has been given to us for the transfiguration is grace. We have received grace for grace. Grace is God's love, power, honor, riches, strength, glory, wisdom, and so much more of His blessings to us, without any contribution on the part of humanity, to merit or earn God's disposition to show such divine favor. It is His unconditional love and compassion towards us to rescue humanity from a fallen creation.

One of the spiritual keys to understanding the mystery of our Sonship is to have our Heavenly Father give us understanding by the Holy Spirit on the vastness of what is encompassed in grace. In the Gospel of John, we see the following declaration inspired divinely by the Spirit of Truth. "And of his fulness have all we received, and grace for grace. For the law was given by Moses, but grace and truth came by Jesus Christ." John 1:16-17

Jesus was also a recipient of the Father's grace. We see in Luke 2:40 "And the child grew, and waxed strong in spirit, filled with wisdom: and the grace of God was upon him." If Jesus operated in grace as the Messiah, then how much more will we have to operate in this grace and Truth to fulfil the plan of God in our lives!

It is necessary to reiterate herein that Jesus stripped Himself of all He had as deity and became a man –thereby joining the human race. Through the one man (Adam) all of creation fell. Through the second Adam (Jesus) all of creation will be made new, and as many as receive Christ will be given power to become the children God. Jesus is the first born in the New Creation. By the grace that was upon His life He has redeemed us, and we will eventually see the redemption of this entire universe. Through the grace that operated in the life of Christ, the Father declared in Revelation 21:5 "And he that sat upon the throne said, Behold, I make all things new. And he said unto me, Write: for these words are true and faithful."

It is by the grace that flourished in the life of Christ and the grace that continues to flourish in the earth by the work of Christ that we will see the fullness of God's plan consummated. Everything starts and ends with our Heavenly Father. Everything starts from His Throne! He is Alpha

Omega. No, I did not say Alpha and Omega. I said He is Alpha Omega because God was working from the beginning and everywhere in between! And He will eventually bring this age to an end! His plan to harvest the precious fruit of the earth is the reason for this great grace that was bestowed upon Christ and now is being bestowed upon His body which is the Church!

Jesus paved the way for the river of grace to flood the earth by paying the debt of sin that kept us separated from the Father. We need to grow in the knowledge of the price that was paid for this grace to rescue us from bondage and shame.

Let's examine grace from our Heavenly Father's perspective. Grace is God's unmerited favor, provision, power, love, and divine ability freely extended to humanity through Christ. There is nothing man can do to merit the favor, compassion, or the mercy of God.

Grace came to us through Jesus Christ. Jesus is the point of reference for the Father when He sends His grace into our lives. However, we as believers can frustrate the grace freely given to us by our Heavenly Father when we, His children, get into a place where we consider we have somehow merited the favor of or affection of Heaven through our own personal righteousness.

After being accepted in the beloved by the blood of Jesus we sometimes are drawn into self-delusion because we feel that we are maintaining a righteous standard by our own ability. We study and memorize Scriptures and we begin to look around to compare ourselves with those who are struggling in the faith, or even those who are lost.

When we make such comparisons, we forget that we are where we are in Christ because God's grace rescued us through Jesus' sacrifice, and it is His grace that brought salvation unto us (by grace through faith are we saved). We also must realize it is His sustaining grace that keeps us, and not we ourselves. Pride is surely the enemy of this lovely grace we have in Jesus. We are lifted up in pride when we entertain the thought that we are now responsible to live a Holy life apart from the lovely grace of God through self-discipline. We find ourselves in the same arena of all the other religions of the world when we attempt to attain right standing before God through fleshly efforts.

All religions proclaim the way to God is to purify yourself by removing habits and behaviors from your lifestyle. Religion teaches that by doing so in self-denial we will somehow gain the approval of a supreme being who will then declare you are good enough to enter his domain and eternal kingdom. This is the great lie and deception of Satan. It is based on the same pride that caused Satan's demise. Satan himself became self-centered and made himself independent from God in his quest to equal himself with God. To say that we ourselves have the ability, independent of His grace, to bring ourselves into right standing with God, is a denial of the grace that has been given freely through Jesus to save the lost. Grace is also given to preserve those who have received the gift of righteousness. Our dependency is upon the true vine who is Jesus, the Christ. To abide in Jesus is to abide in this wonderful grace. Without Him we can do nothing. Flesh and blood cannot inherit the Kingdom, and when we depend on the flesh, we fall from grace.

The Church at Galatia was a blood bought Church. They had received Jesus as Lord. Through wonderful signs and wonders they came into the saving grace and knowledge of Jesus. But not soon after they began to turn to Judaism.

They were being influenced by the teachers of the law instead of the new and living way, which is Christ. These false teachers wanted these newborn Galatians to keep the law. They wanted the Galatians to accept circumcision of the flesh which was *adding* to the work that Christ had already accomplished and finished in His death, burial, and resurrection.

Again, we need to acknowledge the Truth that declares it is grace for grace. So, this is the reason the Apostle Paul wrote under the power of the Spirit this following Truth.

"O foolish Galatians, who hath bewitched you, that ye should not obey the truth, before whose eyes Jesus Christ hath been evidently set forth, crucified among you? This only would I learn of you, Received ye the Spirit by the works of the law, or by the hearing of faith? Are ye so foolish? having begun in the Spirit, are ye now made perfect by the flesh?" Galatians 3:1-3

See also Galatians 5 "Behold, I Paul say unto you, that if ye be circumcised, Christ shall profit you nothing. For I testify again to every man that is circumcised, that he is a debtor to do the whole law. Christ is become of no effect unto you, whosoever of you are justified by the law;

ye are fallen from grace. For we through the Spirit wait for the hope of righteousness by faith. For in Jesus Christ neither circumcision availeth anything, nor uncircumcision; but faith which worketh by love." Galatians 5:2-6

Notice that the Spirit of Truth is negating all previous demands that were put on Israel to keep the law and circumcision to receive the blessing of the Lord. The scripture declares that the blessing has come through the seed of Abraham, which is Christ. And the blessing is by grace through faith.

"For by grace are ye saved through faith; and that not of yourselves: it is the gift of God:" Ephesians 2:8

So, then Jesus redeemed us by grace and sustains us by His grace. He equips us for the ministry by grace, so all is of grace, lest any man should boast. No flesh will ever have grounds to glory in the presence of the living God because it is that grace which came through and by the Lamb, that we have been given all things.

Paul declared the following:

"But by the grace of God I am what I am: and his grace which was bestowed upon me was not in vain; but I labored more abundantly than they all: yet not I, but the grace of God which was with me." 1 Corinthians 15:10

So, what was it that empowered the Apostle Paul to labor more than all the other apostles? It was great grace from the Father of Glory. As we continue in His grace, we will always experience an inward drive and power to do the will of God. We will become more in tune with Heaven and less concerned with the world. Grace will heighten our sensitivity to the things of God and break our attraction to the things of the world. We will declare an addiction for the ministry of Christ. When His grace is allowed free reign in our hearts, then sin, sickness, and poverty will be eradicated.

The grace of our Lord is always available in the lives of God's children. Even in times of trouble, whether we have missed the mark or under pressure from the enemy, we are to boldly go to His Throne to receive grace to help us in times of need.

Hebrews 4:16 says "Let us therefore come boldly unto the Throne of grace, that we may obtain mercy, and find grace to help in time of need."

Our Heavenly Father invites us to come boldly to His Throne to receive grace! If we come in fear, timidity, condemned, or in self-delusion, we insult the supreme sacrifice of Christ. God has not given us a spirit of fear but of power, of love and a sound mind. See 2 Timothy 1:7. We come boldly to His Throne because Jesus paid the full admission and gave us the gift of righteousness! No, we are not coming because of what we earned, but we are coming boldly because Jesus is the new and living way! He paved a way into the Holy of Holies with His blood!

If we attempt to resolve issues or life challenges outside of His grace, then we frustrate the grace of God. We see an example of frustrating God's grace in the Epistle written to the Church at Galatia.

The Galatians began their journey in the Spirit of grace and witnessed the power of God in great manifestation among them. The Apostle Paul wrote of the miracles that had been performed by the Spirit and grace of our Lord. The enemy has no place among believers when we operate in the Spirit of God in partaking of His grace. But if we give place to the enemy by moving away from grace, i.e., receiving religion, legalism, or tradition, while denying the Holy Spirit the freedom to bring in the Law of the Spirit of life releasing a continual flow of God's grace, we will frustrate God's grace. Paul told the Church at Galatia that they had frustrated the grace of God. The Lord Jesus, who is the head of the Church, wants to lord over His Church, imparting grace to all for salvation. We need grace for daily living in the Kingdom as we continue in the earth. We need grace for the work of the ministry that we are called to in the body of Christ.

Specifically, we are all members of the body of Christ, and we all need God's grace to fulfill our calling, no matter our position or station in life. If you are a minister, lawyer, teacher, janitor, parent, or several of the above, God has grace for you. There is no substitute for God's grace and power. When grace is at work God is at work in us, both to will and to do of His good pleasure.

We find ourselves walking in the reality of being more than conquerors in Christ Jesus when grace is abounding in our lives. The Word of God declares we have received the abundance of grace. See Romans 5:17. We reign in life in this grace and operate as heirs together with Jesus. God has designed grace for us, so that we never have to depend, or trust in the flesh, because no flesh will ever glory in His presence. It is the gift of God and not of works. By grace through faith, we have been made citizens in this Kingdom and we are surrounded by His grace and His glory. What a privilege we have in this eternal grace which has been given to the whosoever receives Him; He has given us power to become sons and daughters of God. It is grace for grace.

Even in the Old Covenant it was grace that Noah found in the sight of God to continue and preserve the earth before and after the flood.

There is also grace, to operate in giving into the charities of Heaven. I mean those things that come from and touch the heart of our Father. The Apostle Paul made reference to the grace of giving in 2 Corinthians 8, below:

"Moreover, brethren, we do you to wit of the grace of God bestowed on the churches of Macedonia; How that in a great trial of affliction the abundance of their joy and their deep poverty abounded unto the riches of their liberality. For to their power, I bear record, yea, and beyond their power they were willing of themselves; Praying us with much intreaty that we would receive the gift, and take upon us the fellowship of the ministering to the saints. And this they did, not as we hoped, but first gave their own selves to the Lord, and unto us by the will of God. Insomuch that we desired Titus, that as he had begun, so he would also finish in you the same grace also. Therefore, as ye abound in everything, in faith, and utterance, and knowledge, and in all diligence, and in your love to us, see that ye abound in this grace also. For ye know the grace of our Lord Jesus Christ, that, though he was rich, yet for your sakes he became poor, that ye through his poverty might be rich." See 2 Corinthians 8, *King James Version*

Sometimes as believers we struggle in giving because we are blinded by the lust to have and control our own finances apart from the Lordship of Christ. We find ourselves in anxiety and frustration when it is time to give tithes and offerings to support the ministry of His Kingdom in the earth. The reason for the uneasiness is because we have not been enlightened concerning the grace and Lordship of Jesus when it comes to our finances. We are sometimes serving unrighteous mammon (money), as opposed to God.

When we set our affection on things above and have our fellowship and conversations in Heaven, we operate in a Kingdom reality that lifts us into the grace to give, which comes through Jesus Christ. What a blessing and a divine fulfilment that is released in our hearts when we partake of this grace! We are sowing spiritually and unselfishly by grace, which includes the loving nature of our Father! We become workers together with Him in our giving!

All our labor should be by the grace of our Lord. It is abundant grace, and this grace includes giving. God so loved the world that He gave. This same love and grace will operate in us as we partake of His divine nature that is resident in our new hearts. If any man be in Christ, he is a new creature (creation). We are a new species born of God. We have received the abundance of grace and we should never operate out of the weak and beggarly elements of the flesh.

So we learn by revelation all about this sufficient grace of God. We understand that in every part of our salvation, whether the new birth, healing (spirit, soul, and body) or the abundant provision of God, it is all by grace.

Many Christians would be healed and walking in divine health by this same grace, but instead, they fall short of the glory by attempting to approach God's grace (which provides divine health) on their own merit. Many have worked and served in the church. They have given tithes and offerings. They have assisted the poor and needy so they approach God thinking He should heal them and give divine health based on their works. That is the quickest way to lose out on the blessings of your inheritance because the only way to approach the Father is through the Lamb, and in the Lamb's name, which is Jesus! When we come in the name of Jesus there is grace in abundance because we are acknowledging that Jesus is our grace and Truth. This is the way into all the blessing of the Lord. When we simply rely on the finished work of Jesus Christ, this includes His outpouring into our lives --grace for grace!

Grace is also granted to those who have received the salvation of the Lord to release the favor and blessings of the Lord freely unto all who will receive the Lamb. Without God's grace working in us, through us, and upon us who are the body of Christ, there is no intervention from Heaven into the affairs of men to bring salvation. God so loved the world that He gave us Jesus. When He gave us Jesus, He gave us the full spectrum of His grace. God's grace not only covers all the forces of His goodness on earth, but it also includes all that has been prepared in Heaven for the whole family of God in Heaven and on earth. God's grace is responsible for the exceeding abundance, above all we can ask or think. God's grace is responsible for every blessing we enjoy, which includes everything from the new birth to the promised new earth.

There is so much to consider, because with God's grace working in the believer's life this causes us to reach beyond this three-dimensional finite realm into the eternal-infinite realm of the Kingdom, where we bring divine power into the natural realm; this will manifest the awesome promises, beauty, treasures, glory, and miracles of God. We can only lay hold of the invisible by grace that has been poured into our spirits because of the Lamb. We are spirit men and spirit women who operate in a realm where no impossibilities exist because all is of God. God draws us into continual transfiguration and transformation from one dimension to another. We weep with joy, unspeakable joy, as we partake of the divine nature of our Father, walking in the very weighty presence of the Lord God Almighty.

As we continue in Christ and His Word, we allow God's grace to explode and expand our lives to impact the nations. We operate in God's power by a grace that will destroy the works of the adversary and preserve us blameless before the Throne of Heaven. We are agents of an unchanging God sent to change and reverse all that resulted from the fall of Adam. We are steadfast, unmovable, always abounding in the work of the Lord, as long as we continue in His grace. If we frustrate the grace by resorting to our own ability or righteousness, again, we operate out of the flesh, where therein dwells no good thing. See Romans 7:18a

Prayer

Father, we thank you for Jesus our spotless Lamb who came to bring grace and Truth. Through Him we have received grace for grace. We thank you that this grace and peace are being multiplied in our lives. We thank you for the abundance of grace that has been released in the body of Christ to empower the Church for unfathomable ministry to the nations in this hour. We accept your grace and purpose in fulfilling all you have planned for us as the Church, collectively and individually, in Jesus' Mighty Name! Amen!

Highlights

1. Grace is God's love, power, honor, riches, strength, glory, wisdom, and blessings to us without any contribution on the part of humanity to merit or earn God's disposition, to show such divine favor.

2. Jesus was also a recipient of the Father's grace. We see in Luke 2:40 (Jesus) "And the child grew, and waxed strong in spirit, filled with wisdom: and the grace of God was upon him." If Jesus operated in grace as the Messiah, then how much more we will have to operate in this grace and Truth to fulfill the plan of God in our lives.

3. Many Christians would be healed and walking in divine health by this same grace, but instead, they fall short of the glory by attempting to approach God's grace (which provides divine health) on their own merit.

Reflection & Discussion Questions

1. How is God's grace obtained and who qualifies for it?

2. What is meant by the Scripture in John 1:16 "And of his fulness have all we received, and grace for grace"? Specifically, grace for grace?

3. What is meant by the Scripture in Romans 5:20 that declares where sin abounds does grace much more abound?

Chapter 7

A New Creation

From the foundation of the world God had a plan for man. We know the Word of God says Jesus was crucified from the foundation of the world. The Apostle Paul, under the inspiration of the Holy Spirit, declared the following truth in the Book of Colossians.

"Whereof I am made a minister, according to the dispensation of God which is given to me for you, to fulfil the word of God; Even the mystery which hath been hid from ages and from generations, but now is made manifest to his saints: To whom God would make known what is the riches of the glory of this mystery among the Gentiles; which is Christ in you, the hope of glory:" Colossians 1:25-27 *King James Version*

As the Church continues the transformation and transfiguration in and through Christ, we the Church continue evolving into the fullness of the measure of the stature of Christ. We are constantly being changed into the Father's image and likeness as the body of Christ upon the earth. The Scripture says in Ephesians 1:20 that we might know the power that was wrought when He (God) raised Jesus from the dead. The power that was wrought is invisibly working in all of creation. Immortality is slowly laying hold of mortality because the works of Satan are being demolished and destroyed. There is an eviction notice about to be served to all of darkness. The apostles of the Lamb witnessed the birth and entrance of this New Creation on humanity. Through history we have seen the effects of the Kingdom of His Son on civilizations that have sprung up on every continent, ushering in an eventual renaissance revival in technology, medicine, arts, and music, impacting culture and governments throughout the entire world.

All knowledge comes from God. He is light and His light has brought forth all disciplines in our educational institutions throughout the nations. During the last two centuries we have seen an increase in knowledge that has eclipsed all the previous centuries combined. This knowledge was inspired by God through men who were in deep fellowship with Him. They were inspired to build educational institutions such as Oxford,

Harvard, and Yale. These leading institutions, among many others, have Christ's biblical foundations.

One of the most noted revivals took place on the campus of Yale in 1802. There came, as history calls it, the Second Great Awakening to Yale College. This revival spread throughout the colonies bringing New Creation realities to the hearts of men and changed the culture and morality of the nation. The nature of our Lord so changed communities until the taverns closed and the churches flourished.

During seasons of revivals, on this scale, the Lord of the harvest divinely and supernaturally by His Spirit brings forth a presence of Heaven into the earth that charges the very atmosphere in communities. You will find in studying the awakenings and revivals, not only here in America but also in other nations, such as Germany in the early 1700s and Wales in the 1904 and 1905 era, that there was a manifestation of God's Holy presence that drew churches and communities into the higher realities of God! In such atmosphere, there is no questioning the existence of God and His Kingdom. Humanity is visited with the same power the Apostle Paul experienced on the road to Damascus when he was met by the light and the glory of God in these seasons of awakenings. Such revelations of Christ bring forth a Holy awe in the lives of those visited by the loving King.

There are no words to express what happens in the heart and soul of an individual who is exposed to the power being visited by the Spirit and presence of the Creator of the heavens. Earthly matters are immediately downgraded to the temporal, distracting lower realities that they are, while Heaven becomes the supreme focus of affection to those enjoying the grace and love revealed by Jesus the King.

During times of awakenings to New Creation realities, you will find that God visits the masses at such a level that all intellectual arguments are swept away and replaced by the sobering awe of God's Holy presence. I have had personal encounters with the Lord that are so sacred that my heart begins to gently burn as the men on the road to Emmaus, when they encountered Christ after His resurrection. They declared to one another "…did not our hearts burn in us while He walked with us…?" See Luke 24:32

The Word of God is true. The psalmist declared, taste and see that the Lord is good. The psalmist also declared in His presence there is fullness of joy. Peter declared it joy unspeakable and full of glory. When God shows up in His glory, granting Holy visitations to men, there is a Holy reverence that comes upon the heart that causes one to fall and worship before Him, spontaneously and without coercion! He is the Lord God Almighty, and when He chooses to manifest His glory, it exposes every lie and deception ever manufactured by darkness. When God shows up light shows up because God is light and in Him there is no darkness, neither any shadow of turning. God is light! He is not an earthly or natural light! The light that *God is* carries *all* of who He is, was, and is to come! The light that God released in Genesis 1, He declared light be, and light was, and the darkness comprehended it not, nor prevented it!

God the light gave birth to the New Creation and raised His Son Jesus Christ. It was the light of God that pierced the darkness of hell to raise Jesus from the dead after He paid the awful penalty for all fallen creation. So, Colossians 1:13b declares we have been translated out of the power of darkness into the Kingdom of His Dear Son! This New Creation is the Kingdom that Jesus told the disciples to pray about that would come before His death, burial, and resurrection. When Jesus was raised up an everlasting Kingdom was born. Oh, the rejoicing of Heaven and the angels when Christ and His Kingdom had come to the earth to reign until every enemy has been placed under His body, the Church! He is Conquering King, and we are reigning with Him in this life. I am speaking of those who know and walk in the Truth of His Word!

So, we are not down and out; we are not up and coming; we are reigning in the New Creation with our risen King!

God, by His Spirit, who teaches us all things by His anointing according to 1 John 2:27, has raised up man (male/female) throughout the centuries to enlighten and educate the masses. These individuals were gifted by our Heavenly Father to excel and pioneer the foundations that were needed to inspire learning that would usher in the technologies of this hour. These technologies are lending themselves to propagate (or spread) the Gospel at a rate and speed that serves to complement God's decree that in these last days He would finish the work and cut it short in righteousness, because a short work will the Lord make upon the earth. See Romans 9:28. Knowledge is accelerating in this hour, both on a spiritual and natural level. God has extended life naturally, through medical science, to give humanity every opportunity to receive salvation through His Son Jesus Christ. The Gospel is being preached from every platform and media. Social media, television, radio, and XM satellites. Also, there are apps on phones, tablets and laptops giving humanity access to Christian programing, 24/7. No generation has ever been exposed to truth and light at the level this generation has been exposed. To the demise of many, they have sadly ignored and rejected the only true and living God. They will be judged for rejecting His Son who was sent to save the whole world. As many as received Him (Jesus) gave He power to become the Sons of God. See John 1:12. For those who have received Jesus as King and made Him Lord in this hour, they shall flourish in the courts of the Lord! They have been translated into the New Creation. They are citizens of New Jerusalem! They are reigning with Christ as kings and priests unto God in the earth! See Revelation 1:6. We are the generation that has been called to usher in the second coming of the Lamb! There is an excitement burning in the hearts of those who have come into the living reality of 1 John 1:3 and declare truly that our fellowship is with the Father and His Son Jesus Christ!

We are witnessing and we are a part of this great transfiguration of the body of Christ in the earth. There is fire on the mountain of God in this invisible Kingdom that is about to fall on the nations. Men will declare, as Jeremiah declared "And if I say, I will not make mention of him, nor speak any more in his name, then there is in mine heart as it were a burning fire shut up in my bones, and I am weary with forbearing, and I cannot contain." Jeremiah 20:9 *(English Revised Version)* It is a purging, pruning, transforming fire that will bless the Church, to send it out equipped with divine love and power to reap the harvest in the earth.

As we go forth in the fellowship and work of the Father in His Holy fire, we will be transfigured with light because again, God is light, and it is God's light at work in us both to will and to do of His awesome pleasure! See Philippians 2:13.

Many of the temples and the so-called gods and goddesses were immediately exposed after the death, burial, and resurrection of Christ. These false idols were exposed as the Gospel flowed into Asia, North Africa and, eventually into Europe. Many of those temples are still standing today as historical landmarks, but they no longer serve the cause of darkness because the Light (Jesus, the Christ) has come. The New Creation is here.

In Revelation 1:11, John received revelation concerning the seven churches that were scattered throughout Asia. Satan had set up idolatry strongholds. John, by the power of the Holy Spirit, gave a word of knowledge (current events) concerning the churches in Asia's current state, spiritually. John continued in the Spirit, giving the churches God's word of wisdom (concerning future events) to help those churches gain spiritual traction to advance in God's glory, as they obeyed His instructions, through the challenges of the season they were in.

We see the same Truth is timeless and universal for the Church today. The same challenges the Church faced in the early centuries are the challenges it faces now. The idols are no longer in huge stone and marble temples. The idols of today are bank accounts, education, sex, drugs, entertainment, and many other things that are simply the lust of the flesh, the lust of the eyes and the pride of life.

We are called by His grace to return to our first love as the Church of Ephesus was in Revelation 2:4. Many have abandoned the first love of the Father in this hour. We have been desensitized by the flesh and the sensationalism of this world's system. The Apostle Paul declared the love of some will wax cold in these last days. Any time we separate from the love of God that is shed abroad in our hearts by the Holy Spirit, we break fellowship with the Father. When fellowship is broken, we walk in darkness, and we are no longer walking in His glorious light. The only way back into this wonderful life of fellowship is to quickly repent so we can be restored to fellowship by our High Priest Jesus Christ. 1 John 1:9 declares, "If we confess our sins, he is faithful and just to forgive us our sins, and to cleanse us from all unrighteousness."

We are told by our Father, as a global Church in Revelation 2:8-10, not to fear persecution, imprisonments, tribulation nor death as the Spirit spoke through John concerning the Church at Smyrna. There is strong persecution of the Church in many countries, and we need to be sensitive to the Holy Spirit and give strong intercession daily on their behalf. We offer up spiritual sacrifices in the Spirit, causing a supply of the Spirit to be released in the name of Jesus.

God's angels are dispatched when we intercede for persecuted Christians when we pray! We, through the power of prayer, keep Heaven engaged globally and there will be special rewards for those who yield to the great grace needed to endure in such hard places. The Word declares, whatever we bind on earth will be bound in Heaven. We can touch and agree in prayer and change nations. Jesus said men ought to always pray and not faint. So don't think for a minute that we (you) are at the enemy's mercy because greater is He that is in you than He that is in the world. See 1 John 4:4.

We have grown in the reality of the authority that Christ has given the Church over the centuries. We are no longer ignorant of our weaponry, nor Satan's devices. We have been given the complete written Word of God, and we are no longer illiterate naturally or spiritually. We are equipped and empowered by Almighty God, the Creator of the universe, who happens to be our Daddy!

We give ourselves completely over to our Heavenly Father for His use in this hour to be continuously filled with His power. We consecrate to His call. There will be rewards for those who give themselves sacrificially, denying themselves the pleasures of this world and presenting their bodies to God --praying sometimes hours to God for the persecuted Church and for the harvest of the nations.

The reason the enemy sends persecution is to stop the spread of this glorious Gospel and the precious fruit of the earth. But the gates of hell will not prevail! No weapon formed against us will prosper! Nothing will stop this mighty move of God! His all-sufficient grace will always turn our weakness into strength! Nothing will separate us from the love of God, and His love never fails! It will not fade out nor come to an end! Love's hopes are fadeless and endures all things without weakening! It is Christ being glorified in our mortal bodies! We are more than conquerors in all these things through Christ who loved us and gave Himself for us! The Church always flourishes during persecution, even in the midst of being used as entertainment in the Roman coliseums. God caused Rome to be turned from a barbaric blood-thirsty people to an empire that was drawn into Christianity. It was the power of the Gospel. It was Christ, and His body, the Church, filled with the hope of glory that prevailed! We shall reign in the earth with Christ until every enemy has been made His footstool. It is not by might nor by power but by my Spirit saith the Lord. See Zechariah 4:6.

Again, all of the seven churches in Revelation, Chapters 2 and 3 were given instructions by God to lift the Church beyond the gravitational pull of the world system and persecution so they could continue in the transfiguration/transformation that is soon to reach its zenith. The

94

Church, over the centuries, has been changed, chastened, pruned, and transformed so that the fullness of the measure of the stature of Christ will be seen in her before the return of the King of Glory.

We see the vision of Daniel hundreds of years in advance in the 2nd Chapter of the Book of Daniel, concerning the giant statue made of gold, silver, bronze, iron, and clay, representing the empires that were to stand prior to the coming of Christ. Jesus was the stone cut out of the mountain in the vision. The Babylonian, Neo Persian, Grecian, and Roman empires were all destroyed in the vision being represented by the giant. God gave King Nebuchadnezzar of the Babylonian empire a dream that troubled him. So, he sent for the wise men and astrologers to tell him or interpret for him, what he had dreamed. The wise men and astrologers were the so-called learned men of the day. But they informed King Nebuchadnezzar that they could not interpret the dream without being told the dream. The King was furious and commanded that all the wise and learned men be executed immediately. Daniel asked for time to pray to seek the Lord concerning the dream because he was God's prophet, and he had the Spirit of excellence upon him because of the calling of God for that season.

God has likened men for this hour. We, as born-again believers, exceed where Daniel and all the prophets, kings and priests were in their relationship with the Lord. We are the New Creation. When the power of God raised Jesus from the dead there came forth a Kingdom.

All Old Testament servants held one of the above three offices and they were spiritually dead because the New Creation was not made available until after the finished work of Christ. none these men or women in the Old Testament were baptized into Christ. They simply had the Spirit of God come upon them to operate in the office they were called to. They were the only ones who heard from God. All of Israel had to hear from the man of God to hear from Heaven. But under this new and better Covenant, under the New Creation we are all born of God! We all know God because He lives in us! We are His temple! We can boldly approach His Throne at any time! We don't need the prophet, priest or king! We don't need the pastor, prophet, evangelist, apostle, or teacher to go to the Throne for us, necessarily. We have a direct line to the Throne. We are born of God! We are joined unto the Lord! We are one Spirit with the Lord! We are the manifested children of the Lord! We have been translated out of the power of darkness into the Kingdom of His Dear

Son! We are His offspring! Jesus is the first born of many brethren! The Word declares in 1 John 3:1 "Behold what manner of love the Father has bestowed upon us that we should be called the sons of God!" Hebrews 2:11 declares Jesus is the first born of many brethren! We are the redeemed of the Lord! We are His workmanship! It is God who is at work in us to will and to do of His good pleasure! We are the temple of God, living stones fitly joined together, Jesus Christ being the Chief Corner Stone! We are a habitation built up together with Christ to be inhabited by God! That's why the transfiguration will take place in Christ's body here on the earth, in these final hours as it was transfigured on that mount when Moses and Elijah appeared. It is God in us bringing us, by the Holy Spirit, from one dimension to another, transforming us into His glory and His likeness. We have seen the paintings of saints who lived in centuries passed with a halo around their heads. These were consecrated men and women of God who manifested some level of this glory that is still building in the earth. But stay tuned, for the Church will manifest God's glory at levels that will baffle the world and leave them in Holy awe of His manifestations. This is the glory and the transfiguration that will produce the awesome end time harvest!

The Church is about to explode in light throughout the whole earth! All nations will be hit with tsunami waves of glory! The Buddhist will see Christ; the Hindu will see Christ; the Muslims will see Christ and Israel will see the Messiah! There will be wonderful, glorious manifestations and salvations throughout the earth! This glorious Gospel will have been preached by the transfigured Church, and then will come the end!

This New Creation that is invisible will have reaped a mighty harvest of new creatures from the earth! It is the harvest that God has so patiently waited for! Through all the works of darkness, since the fall of creation, He has patiently waited! Now the stage has been set for this New Creation to swallow up death and all of fallen creation, because God has said in Revelation 21:5 "...Behold I make all things new..." The Apostle John said in Revelation 21:1-3, "And I saw a new heaven and a new earth: for the first heaven and the first earth were passed away; and there was no more sea." And I John saw the holy city, new Jerusalem, coming down from God out of heaven, prepared as a bride adorned for her husband. And I heard a great voice out of heaven saying, Behold, the tabernacle of God is with men, and he will dwell with them, and they shall be his people, and God himself shall be with them, and be their God."

The King is coming! He is still the God who answers by fire! Peter said the old creation will melt with fervent heat! It is the Holy Spirit that will rain down fire in these final days! It is the New Creation coming into full fruition!

Prayer

Father we say come even now Lord Jesus! Let your glory fill us, your temple. Let the revival fire fall on us! Send forth the latter and former rain! Let your manifested glory fill the earth as the waters cover the sea. Draw us into a deeper richer fellowship that we may stand in awe of your goodness and your glory! We yield our members to righteousness unto holiness! We are your vessels of honor, and we declare we are the redeemed! It is in the name of Jesus that we pray! Amen!

Highlights

1. We come into the earth and it is spiritually occupied by those who are born of God. We are citizens of His Kingdom.

2. Through history we have seen the effects of the Kingdom of His Son on civilizations that have sprung up on every continent, ushering in an eventual renaissance revival in technology, medicine, arts, music, impacting culture and governments throughout the entire world.

3. God is light and in Him there is no darkness. He is not natural light. He is the eternal, Heavenly Light!

Reflection & Discussion Questions

1. What is the purpose of the Kingdom of God's Son in the earth?

2. What has to happen to the spirit of those who are lost prior to being accepted into the New Creation?

3. What has to happen to the Church on the earth before it is caught up to God. What measure and stature must it achieve?

www.ingramcontent.com/pod-product-compliance
Lightning Source LLC
Chambersburg PA
CBHW072008060426
42446CB00042B/2253